NORTHAMPTONSHIRE

Edited by Allison Dowse

First published in Great Britain in 2003 by
YOUNG WRITERS
Remus House,
Coltsfoot Drive,
Peterborough, PE2 9JX
Telephone (01733) 890066

HB ISBN 1 84460 008 4
SB ISBN 1 84460 009 2

FOREWORD

This year, the Young Writers' The Write Stuff! competition proudly presents a showcase of the best poetic talent from over 40,000 up-and-coming writers nationwide.

Young Writers was established in 1991 and we are still successful, even in today's modern world, in promoting and encouraging the reading and writing of poetry.

The thought, effort, imagination and hard work put into each poem impressed us all, and once again, the task of selecting poems was a difficult one, but nevertheless, an enjoyable experience.

We hope you are as pleased as we are with the final selection and that you and your family continue to be entertained with *The Write Stuff! Northamptonshire* for many years to come.

CONTENTS

Charlotte Brander	87
Daniel Clements	87
Carron Barnes	88
Laura Courtney	88
Christopher Cosentino	89
Sam Brentegani	89
Abigail Dawes	90
Daniel Grocott	90
Sally Ronch	91
Darren Mann	91
Nicholas Kitchen	92
Victoria Statham	92
Daniel Havard	93
Nickie Gisdakis	93
Natasha Fakih	94
Hannah Carlill	94
Hannah Davis	95
Claire Healey	95
Heidi McKay	96
Adam Robson	96
Roxanne Davis	97
Gemma Berrill	97
Kirsten Wright	98
Abbie Thomas	98
Rachel Vicars	99
Grace Thorne	100
Laurel Atkinson	101
Stephen North	101
Siobhan Moll	102
Ashley Davis	102
Katie Moss	103
Julie Manning	103
Abigail Suthers-Fox	104
Liam Hammond	104
Mark Thompson	105
Catherine Hutter	105
Matthew Payne	106
Aimee Roberts	106

Stella Clarke	107
Adrian Biggins	107
Tom Lenton	108
Neil Black	108
Lilian Lau	109
Carly Brewer	109
Chris Hayward	110
Alex Payne	110
Benjamin Bain	110
Hannah Iddon	111
Joshua Flynn	111
Scott Weaving	111
Lewis Hopper	112
Jamie Cleaver	112
Carlie Morgan	112
Thomas Orcherton	113
Victoria Stickings	113
Louiza White	114
Jamie Smith	114
Clare Gray	115

Lodge Park Technology College

Shaun Franklin	115
William Hadden	116
Jamie Cross	116
Siobodan Manojlovic	116
Joshua Weston	117
Graham Abraham	118
Aarron Young	119
Luke Robinson	119
Emilly Savage	120
Michelle Kingsnorth	121
Jamie Haynes	121
Danielle Macleod	122
Sam McKinnon	122
Kieren Burt	123
Zoe Wood	124
Remi McNeill	124

Joe Doherty	150
Sarah King	150
Keri Bethel	151
Ashleigh Burrows	151
Katie Dickson	152
Colin McGreevy	152
Daryl Veal	153
Lucy Mackenzie	153
Paul Britton	154
April Jackson	154
Mark Burton	155
Ryan Stewart	155
Nicola Howden	156
Joanne Beaton	156
Alexander Lyon	157
Hayley Muir	157
Gail Sheridan	158
Dusan Knezevic	158
Katie Jones	159
Carly Black	159

Manor School

Leanne Booth	159
Ian Flanagan	160
Chris Ovenden	160
Karen Britchford	161
Charlotte Johnson	162
Kathryn Wieczorek	162
Charlotte Bramble	163
Jemmer Parnell	164
Oliver Tatum	164
Jack Maddix	165
Natalie Medforth	166
David Smith	166
Kayley Dickens	167
Emma Dixon	168
Emma Yates	168
Luke Beardmore	169

The Poems

WHAT WILL HAPPEN WHEN I TURN 13?

What will happen when I turn 13?
At 12 midnight will my hair turn green?
Will I get spots all over my face?
Will I endanger the human race?

Will I pierce my eyebrows and tongue?
Will heavy metal music be sung?
Will I change my moods every day?
Will I be angry with everything I say?

Will I be shouting at my mum?
Will doors be slammed and banged as I come?
Will I shout at my brother?
Will we dislike one another?

Will I be obsessed with how I look?
Will I want the haircut from the book?
Will I take make-up from a handy case
And then apply it to my face?

Will I go out to a disco all night?
Get back to have a fight?
Shouting and screaming everywhere?
No place of love and care?

Will I stamp and shout and roar
Upstairs to slam my door?
Will my eyes stare with an evil beam?
What will happen when I turn 13?

Sarah Jane Elliott (12)
Bishop Stopford School

COLD STREETS OF LONDON

Nothing have I
Begging to stay alive,
Ground is as hard as nails
Rubbish and grime around.
Rain pounds on me like bullets
Soaking to the ground.
The wind ran through the streets,
Howling as it came.
Angry as people looking down
Feeling invisible.
The city smells of smoke,
Buildings crowd me in,
Miserable
As people go past,
I am like dirt,
Cold, damp and sick, this is what I am.
As I sleep, I wish for morning.

Andrew Kingsnorth (13)
Bishop Stopford School

LOST IN SPACE

I have been alone, cold, damp and lost
Gutters and doorways, my only friends.
Am I invisible, someone to forget?
A couple of coppers per day, that's all I get.

You see things on TV, so awful, so wrong
I live that sitcom through and through.
Glaring tramps, grinding teeth
Why doesn't Hell let me in?

Sleep, what does that mean?
Haven't had that for weeks.
Bruises, black and blue
The only colours I know.

My clothes, they smell
My stubble uncut
I am just a piece of rubbish
To forget about or throw away.

Rachael Nutt (14)
Bishop Stopford School

INVISIBLE

The days drag past slowly,
Day in, day out,
Nothing ever changes.

The floor bites into me, it's as cold as ice,
The wind pulls and pushes me like I'm its slave,
I often think, *why me?*
What have I done to deserve the punishment of cold, dusty doorways?
And the hunger eats me up inside till nothing is left, it's so painful.

People just walk by like you're not there,
You're as invisible as a shadow,
A fly on the wall to ignore,
That's when you realise nobody cares and nobody ever will,
Because as far as they're concerned, it's your fault you're sitting
In a cold dusty doorway,
That's me - invisible!

Chloe Hignett (13)
Bishop Stopford School

LOST

I am lonely and cold,
Sore and lost,
Leaves falling,
I'm calling,
Calling for desperate help to stop
                    this endless pain,
Time goes by like an everlasting war,
People shoot by like a train that is late,
I am a freak in a circus,
I am garbage,
I am nothing,
I am a lost image that never was to be,
Darkness and winter have come,
Twelve pence is all I had
From a day's scrounge,
'Not bad?'
What a lie!
I just felt cheap,
I am hungry and thirsty,
Sad and in pain,
Floating away unnoticed.

Paul Roberts (13)
Bishop Stopford School

DOSSING ALL DAY

My hands are frozen like ice,
My toes are whiter than icecaps,
My back is sore,
Because I'm dossing all day.

My hat is scattered with coppers,
My bag is empty with nothing,
My legs are sore,
Because I'm dossing all day.

My sleeping bag is crowded with me,
My pockets are filled with dust,
My head is sore,
Because I'm scrounging all day.

Christian Ruppnig (13)
Bishop Stopford School

AN ICY GRAVEYARD

Dismal, dark and destructive,
Are the cold nights of winter,
And as we sit upon a scarlet carpet of snow,
We admire war's good work.
The voices of the optimists howl emptily through the air.
'Hope?'
Icy tears roll down our expressionless faces,
And as we gaze over the sparse meaningless landscape,
I see the injured, limping like inebriated fools.
The bodies of great friends, soulless in the icy depths,
And the trees blowing in a cutting wind.

'Hark the Herald,' a centurion voice bellows among the groans
of the wounded,
But, one gunshot later, his body joins the soulless dead,
His songs disappearing into the dark depths of the night.

Why? I ask myself,
This is not necessary
But, as I say this, another innocent man is slain,
Sending my thoughts into a meaningless world.

I would never wish this upon anyone,
This torture we've endured
And in the future I wish no one to pay a visit to those battlefields:
That icy hell.

Tom Holman (14)
Bishop Stopford School

THIS IS LIFE

I'm lying here in a doorway,
Cold, hungry and lonely.
The streetlight is shining on me,
I feel like a clown everyone is laughing and
pointing at.
This is life!

I'm sitting here scrounging and dossing,
Cold, hungry and lonely.
This isn't the way it should be,
I feel like a dirty fly that everyone wants to swat.
This is life!

I'm holding my hands out begging for change,
Cold, hungry and lonely.
The wind is cutting into me,
I feel like a vase shattered into millions of pieces.
This is life!

Kathleen Keenan (13)
Bishop Stopford School

ALL ALONE

Being homeless is no walk in the park,
The rain smacks the ground and becomes a river.
The wind chases me to make me colder,
The ground is like solid metal with big spikes.

I watch people go by,
I ask for money, all you get is, 'No!'
They are like monsters that are going to eat you.

My hunger eats into me,
Like a tiger tearing into me.
I look like a scruffy dog
And I smell terrible.

All alone now!
I feel depressed, rejected, most of all, isolated.
I want to see my mum,
I want her to make me feel special again.

Jay Mashari (13)
Bishop Stopford School

JUST A DREAM?

Out in the cold,
Never-ending nights;
Long days,
Sky, deadly to homeless;
Engulfed by preying darkness,
Destroyed by painful rain,
Vulnerable as a small child
Trapped by attacking wind,
Frozen as icy snowcaps
Lost in a bewildered world,
Hapless in a contemptible planet,
Left to a lifeless Earth,
Hidden in a shabby hole,
Death around every corner,
Silence!

Wendy Allen (13)
Bishop Stopford School

LIFE

The numbness and the loneliness keeps you locked in a rusty cage,
No door, no key, no escape,
Trees hit me with their scaly leaves and arms,
I need peace, but people crash into me like tidal waves
                                        crashing on a beach of clones,
Us,
The street people,
The people that are bitten by the wind as others retreat to their
                                        roaring fires and central heating,
I am as free as the wind,
But as trapped as a dog,
I am invisible, but people see me,
Sitting on my own in solitude,
In pain,
Pain inside me
And all I know is,
I am one of them too,
I am homeless!

Anna Wills (13)
Bishop Stopford School

GOLDEN

The meadow is shrouded in mist
Until the sun comes up like a golden fist.

It creates long, golden shimmering grass with golden dew
Like golden glass.

Golden flowers, big and small
Create a beautiful golden wall.

A golden horse eats golden grass
As a golden stream drifts slowly past.

A golden morning, fresh and bright,
Transforms the darkness of the night.

George James (13)
Bishop Stopford School

ME

Here I am
In a doorway sitting,
Waiting.
For what?
Food, water, death.
The people of the town swish past me like a wave from the sea
I am a shipwreck that the other ships look down on
I am as frozen as a block of ice
But,
No one knows and nobody cares
My hunger haunts me while my thirst seduces me.
This concrete on which I sit is nailing me to its stony, sharp, freezing
surface and there's no way it will let me go
I am trapped. No!

I am homeless.

Jade Gardiner (13)
Bishop Stopford School

LOST

What's it like to be homeless?
You'll probably ask
And there aren't words to prepare you for
The terrible sights you'll see
The foul things you'll smell
And the thoughts you think
And that's the honest truth.

I smell as rotten as a dustbin
I look as disgraceful as a flea-bitten dog
I feel like a piece of rubbish

Nothing, that's what I am
I feel invisible
I am homeless.

Beth Tracey (13)
Bishop Stopford School

TIGERS

Mouth full, munching
When a tiger eats his prey.
Then ready to rest for the day.

Ripping rapidly
Tearing his prey apart
Eating and ripping its heart.

Helping hunters
When he calls for help
When a tiger spots him.

Licking lively
After having his lunch
Using his axe-like claws.

Sleeping soundly
Don't you do it too,
Because you never know,
      he might be after you!

Steven Jones (12)
Bishop Stopford School

MORE TO EARTH

There's more to Earth than green and blue
And more to Earth than race,
With black and white,
There's hope in sight,
The future needs our grace.

There's more to Earth than anger
And more to Earth than sorrow,
With brother and son,
To lean upon,
Let's save these kids of tomorrow!

There's more to Earth than trees and plants,
And more to Earth that's great,
As countryside dies,
Time hides the lies
And later is always too late.

Sarah Spikesley (12)
Bishop Stopford School

MY WORLD

Welcome to my world
It's not very much
I live on the streets
I always look rough.

I am a piece of rubbish
People ignore me as they pass
Sometimes I believe
I'm an outcast.

I am as cold as ice
Lying here on the floor
People shout abuse at me,
'Get out from in front of my door!'

'Any spare change?'
Is what I say,
'No!' is their reply
They're the same every day.

No one wants to be near me
Even the wind pushes me down
With his cold palms
I fall onto the ground.

My life is not exciting,
I hate it through and through
I wish I was somewhere warm
Can't there be something I can do?

Welcome to my world
It's not very much
I live on the streets
I always look rough.

Hannah Elliott (13)
Bishop Stopford School

IS THE PAST THE FUTURE?

My body is frozen
Sadly this is the life I wouldn't have chosen
I feel like rubbish
Chilled to the bone
I'm all alone

Everyday life goes on
I realise I have no one
The wind is biting my toes
And rippling through my moth-eaten clothes

I have no name
Passport or ID
Empty as my heart, I have nobody.

Rebecca Smith (13)
Bishop Stopford School

OUR TORTURED SUN

As gravity pulled, pulled, pulled,
The spherical furnace scattered rays of frustration
in each direction.
He blinded each good soul with his photons of hate,
Piercing them with the intensity of his passion.

But the real anguish was within:
In the very core of his being.
And as gravity sucked in his hate,
He destroyed himself with pain.

Owen Cain (17)
Bishop Stopford School

SPACEWEATHER.COM

I enter . . . Spaceweather.com

I type, what's the weather like in space?
Reply, much darker than in your space.
I type, 'what's there in the weather of space?
Reply, more than what is in your space.

I click on an item on the toolbar,
I see the Leonid meteors are coming from far.
I press spacebar,
It doesn't take me far.

I look on the statistics,
The speed of the solar wind is 392km per second-ics.
There is no fix,
The speed that ticks.

I scroll down to the end of the page,
I read, 'The alien's complaint on his wage.'
The sun is going through a phase,
It always gets its way.

For more Spaceweather information, re-lease,
Outlook Express and e-mail us on
Space@weather.com p-lease.
There are no fee-s
Which is cheaper than going to Greece.

Ruby Bhavra (17)
Bishop Stopford School

IN THE GUTTER

I walked down the floodlit streets of London,
Until I reached a dead end,
When he spotted me,
I tried to run
And succeeded
And sat in a shop entrance.

The pavement was so cold, like me in a way,
It hurt like nothing before,
I knew by now that I wouldn't make 15.

It's the morning, I kept thinking,
As a person walked past me,
They gave me a look as if to say I was garbage
And then I continued,
Into the next day.

Sam Dixey (13)
Bishop Stopford School

ALONE

Life on the street is a horrific thing.
The doorways are gaping jaws waiting for you.
Endless nights drag on.
The ground never lets up on your spine.
Small footsteps scare you into submission.
The wind howls its own tune sending shivers into your spine.
Each day people begrudgingly give you small change.
You get food but only enough to fight on.
Time makes you realise that,
Death is the only way out.

Andrew Etherton (13)
Bishop Stopford School

DREAMS OF LIGHT IN A PLACE OF DARKNESS
(Based on a section of the book 'Goodnight, Mr Tom')

Sweet memories,
They run so deep,
Away from the darkness,
Where shadows creep.
A smile yet,
A weathered face,
Grey-bristled beard,
Once-loved Place.
Away from the hardship,
In the country fair,
Oh how my heart,
Yearns to be there!
The fire burns,
The ash swirls and flies,
The tears are still falling,
From my cobwebbed eyes.
A crack of cold leather,
Agony, pain,
Even in shadow,
I'm there again.
I am trapped in darkness,
A prisoner of war,
Love is what I'm needing,
Like I had before.
My heart is still pining,
My road to death is long,
But forever I will be thinking,
Of dear old Mr Tom . . .

Kirsty Burrows (13)
Bishop Stopford School

PLAYING WITH FIRE

Glowing and burning brightly,
Such are the ways of the fire,
Giving warmth to all around it,
Burning with strong desire.

Fire is quick in spreading,
Once it starts, there's no return,
The fire grows on depending,
On those it needs to burn.

Suddenly you realise what you pay,
For what seemed like fun and games,
As danger engulfs you
And you are overcome with flames.

Furiously the fire burns on,
Destroying everything in its path,
The pillars of flames rise to the sky,
As the fire releases its wrath.

The heavens now open up
And down the water pours,
The chance to carry on with life,
Is, for the moment, yours.

The fire is almost over,
The heat is dying away,
Hope is where despair once was,
It's the dawn of a brand new day.

The fire has turned to ashes,
In the future again it shall spout,
You are filled with eternal happiness,
For the fire is finally out.

Amelia Jane Wilson (13)
Bishop Stopford School

JUST LIKE ME

Cold, icy, is the floor,
Dirty, filthy, am I,
Like the rubbish rolling down the road.
Is this the life I want?
No!
The hunt none of us can run or hide from.
The wolves chase me every morning,
Never leaving,
They tear through me like a knife.
People don't care,
Looking at me like the mouldy sandwich opposite.
I am rubbish.
I am a castaway.
A cast-off piece of society,
Someone with no cause.
It will soon be my turn.
I pull my blanket tightly around my shoulders,
I close my eyes,
I think
Of my mother,
My sister
And dad.
The Grim Reaper has come,
He has come for me,
A perfect choice,
Nobody will notice.
Soon everyone will be slain,
You can't run and you can't hide.
Soon you will lie down on hard stone,
Just like me.

David Carter (13)
Bishop Stopford School

RED

Once a young boy said,
'I hate blue, but I like red.'
As he stared at the sky
an old man passing by
said, 'You young fool. If you wish the sky to be red
then prepare to be dead and dead, dead, dead!'
'Why?' said the boy with a horrified look,
so the man answered, 'Never looked at a book,
bound in history, science and things?
Before humans and others knew how to sing,
before deer or hare or large brown bear,
the sky was red, but had no air.
But I shall give you one last clue,
when air is together it's blue, blue, blue.
'My lad,' he said with a grin,
as though he had been at a bottle of gin,
'if the sky turns that colour that we call red,
prepare to have life ended, to be dead, dead, dead.'

Abigail Vitiello (13)
Campion School

FIRE

Fire is a cat
Long and colourful
It is sometimes playful and sometimes nasty.
In a playful mood the flames can be warming
Friendly pounces and rises
In a nasty mood it can squeal, hiss, spark and spit
It claws up and the flames burn away houses and trees
In a sleepy mood it is calm and slow
It creeps and then sleeps.

Jenna Walker (13) & Michelle Hall (14)
Corby Community College

THE WIND

The wind is an angry leopard,
Climbing through the trees,
It runs through all the countries.
It roars at all the other animals
It's fierce and dangerous when it's angry.
It's angry and powerful.
It's the most dangerous animal in the world.
When the wind is a playful leopard,
It plays with the leaves just like a cat plays with its toys
When the wind is a playful leopard
It's not dangerous, it's funny,
Friendly and nice.
The wind is gentle and is a leopard
It can be sleepy, dangerous or playful.
When the wind is a leopard
It's scary when it's angry.

Kerry McCartney (14)
Corby Community College

FIRE

Fire is a tiger,
Dangerous and hot,
With its yellow, orange and red.
Its teeth and claws are to be feared,
It kills anything in its way,
People, buildings, everything is its prey.

It spits and jumps around,
All day long it bounces off the ground.
Playing with and patting its food,
Everything is good.

When tired, it turns a colour of amber,
It stops its killing building clamber
Everything below is now destroyed
Everything above is unharmed.
Now the fire has stopped, everyone and everything
                                        is saved.

Stacey Allan (13)
Corby Community College

THE WIND

The wind is a wolf,
Roaring with rage,
Pushing down trees,
Howling in ears.

The wind feels playful,
Travelling up people's clothes,
Striking them down,
Whacking with its tail.

The wind is a wolf,
Picking up leaves,
shaking them about,
Dropping them down.

When it feels sleepy,
It falls slow and gentle,
The grass keeps swaying,
Wherever it goes.

But finally it's asleep
And the wind is gone,
Now we can all
Be nice and calm.

Nicola McHarg (13)
Corby Community College

THE WIND

The wind is two mighty horses,
One a calm cool mare,
The other a furious stallion
That mangles and destroys.

The mare cools weary travellers.
Relaxes hot sunbathers.
She opens her mouth and plays with children
By blowing their kites.

The stallion kicks away at trees and homes
With the greatest of ease
And stomps forests with hooves and rage.

But when they meet, all is calm.
Then a mighty hurricane of the two winds
Racing around each other.
The mare in the centre, calm and cool,
The stallion raging around the outside, full of anger.

Adam Gardiner (13)
Corby Community College

WIND

The wind is a lion
Pouncing on its prey
Howling with a roar
While the trees *sway, sway, sway*

Each day he flaps his tail
To wash away the leaves
He jumps up with his claws
Above his head
And pounces on the trees

But when the wind is quiet
And all the leaves are gone
He creeps around the town
Lightly on his paws
Whistling in the cans
While sharpening his claws.

Vicky Black (13)
Corby Community College

WIND

The wind is a hungry dog
It howls
It growls
It moans
And it groans,
It snaps the trees and chases
The leaves.

It skips the leaves across
The road
And plays with the litter
With its nose.
It slams the windows with
Its tail
And flutters the flags in
Its trail.

When it's dark and the puppy's
Shattered,
All he can manage is a little breeze
That waves the top of
The trees.

Mark Bannigan (13)
Corby Community College

THE WIND IS AN EAGLE

The wind is a bold eagle
Causing a blast
The eagle is free
Flying overhead

Hour upon hour he travels
He brushes the trees with his wings
The eagle glides over leaves
Making an autumn day
When the sky is clear he takes a long break

When the eagle whistles
And the bright moon is out
He breathes softly and moves the clouds
The bright moon reflects in his eyes
His eyes close slowly around midnight

By the time it turns May he rests
The eagle has no time for energy
He's too busy building up for winter
He lies down gently resting his wings
He just moves the mid-May clouds.

Samantha Jackson (13)
Corby Community College

WIND

Wind is a raging horse,
Galloping towards you,
Showing its powerful white teeth.

With thunderous hooves
And howling noises,
Scaring everything in its way.

With its powerful tail and manc,
Smashing and crashing,
Lashing things with its tail.

When asleep,
You can't hear a thing,
Just the slight movements in the trees,

But when awake, boy, you will know!

James Lewis (13)
Corby Community College

WIND

The wind is a fierce panther
Giant and black,
He searches, longing for food all day
Clawing at scraps with his paws,
                maybe a human or two.

He rushes quickly and swiftly,
He catches his prey,
He whirls round and round, a hurricane,
In hope to kill it.

He ruffles the grass with his claws,
Crouches down, paws ready,
He pounces towards you
His tail swishes past.

He is now in a slumber
Curled in a bundle,
Shaking lightly, the leaves on a tree,
Breathing softly, a gentle breeze.

Clare Porch (14)
Corby Community College

THE WIND IS AN EAGLE

The wind is an eagle
Soaring through the sky
In and out the trees using his talons
                    to take the leaves hostage
Using his powerful wings to smuggle you away.

Then, all at once he's up your shirt
From the top of your spine to the tips of your toes
Screeching his noises as he surfs the clouds

He frees his hostages and watches them play
Jumping about and dancing away
As he watches them his eyes glow, glow and glow.

Joe McCue (14)
Corby Community College

RUMBLY TUMMY

When he wakes up, he's hungry
And as he stumbles up with his tummy rumbly,
He walks outside and climbs some trees
And after a while he follows some bees,
He follows them off to their home
And empties out their yellow dome,
When he gets home he sways from side to side
Slower than the lapping of the tide.
A bear of very little brain,
Eats so much honey, he's in pain.
No matter what
Christopher Robin loves him.

Polly Harris (13)
Daventry William Parker School

MY MAGIC BOX
(Based on 'The Magic Box' by Kit Wright)

I shall put in my box . . .
The whistle of a singing bluebird
The growls of a sleepy lion
And the smell of the freshest flowers.

I shall put in my box . . .
The biggest chocolate factory there ever is
And the hiss of the angriest dancing dragon.

I shall put in my box . . .
The weirdest alien from munching Mars
Three hundred wishes from the genie
And the biggest sandcastle on the yellowest beach.

I shall put in my box . . .
The smiles of my best friends
Memories of my first birthday
And the twinkle of the wishing star.

I shall put in my box . . .
A multicoloured cat and a black rainbow
The sound of a tap running
And the man jogging up and down the street.

My box is magical in every possible way
From Santa Claus to Mickey Mouse!

I shall read in my box
Dance in my box
And eat in my box
So I shall never ever get bored in life.

Charlotte Craner (13)
Daventry William Parker School

THE MAGICAL STAR

There was a magical star
That sparkled over the night
With its golden glow
It was a sign of God.

There was once a person called James
He saw the sparkling gold race through the night sky
With its golden glow
He wished his ultimate dream.

There was a magical star
That shone over the dark, twisted night
With its golden glow
It was a sign of happy life

There was once a person call Thomas
He watched the gold of light shoot
With its golden glow
His life was a sign.

There was a magical star
That sparkled over the night sky
With its golden glow
It was a sign of a beautiful life

There was a person called Kirsty
She watched the sparkles of gold race
                        through the bright moon
With its golden glow
She was with her dreamed boyfriend

There was a magical star
That sparkled over the night
With its golden glow
It was a sign of God

The magical star twisted on the dark night
It sparkled all the way
With its golden glow
It was the magical star of life.

Chris Amery (14)
Daventry William Parker School

MARS AND THE STARS

I like the stars
I would also like to live on Mars
Have you ever paid attention to the stars?

I have and that's why I like the stars,
But what about Mars?
I like Mars too,
But not forgetting the stars.

If I could live on Mars,
Then I'd have to bring the stars
Then I'd live on Mars, with the stars.

I would like that,
To live on Mars with the stars.

Mars is like distant red eyes watching us
Stars are the factories of the universe
They throw Heaven's dust on.

I'd like to orbit Mars in a car made of stars
Fantastically fast, faster than words.

What if stars and Mars were mixed up in a bag?
Then what would we call the stars and Mars?

Abigail Thompson (13)
Daventry William Parker School

SPACE

The man was up near the stars,
He did not realise he was on Mars.
It was then he saw a fantastic shape,
It was peculiar-looking just like an ape.
Even though it was the summer season,
Up there it was still quite freezing.

Then he spotted the moon,
Which was shaped just like a baboon.
Then he flew right out of space,
With a cold, red, rosy face.
He was out of breath when he hit Earth
Then he had a phone call saying his wife
was giving birth.

Higgledy-piggledy, he ran through everybody,
Then quickly got a teddy bear, Noddy.
This was for his new baby girl or boy.
What else was he to get but a nice cuddly toy?

Nichola Roberts (14)
Daventry William Parker School

CHRISTMAS

Tonight is Christmas Eve
everybody is waiting to receive
a gift from their families
or even Santa Claus.

My stocking is waiting
on the bottom of my bed
by the side of it
is my favourite teddy, Ted.

I hope Christmas will be here soon
I cannot wait till that day comes
when Christmas Day is here.

I'm going to my bed now
I'm really, really excited
over goes my duvet cover
till the morning when
I see the snowflakes flying.

Andrea Green (11)
Daventry William Parker School

MY BEST FRIEND

My friend is not a human being
Or a thing in space,
He is quite simply round the bend
I call him Deefer Dog
He goes mad out in the garden
He goes mad inside the house
He is complete bonkers
I call him Deefer Dog
He loves the windy weather
And he hates the pouring rain
He dances when it's frosty
I call him Deefer Dog
Deefer Dog is my best friend
You can't wish for another
He's always there when I am sad
My dog is like no other.

Deefer!

Rebekah Jane Holloway (13)
Daventry William Parker School

SNOW GLOW!

I wish it would snow, snow
Make the clouds glow
I look at the moon
It's a big fat balloon
The stars at night
A sparkling delight
I look at the sun in the morning
While I am yawning
Wishing it would snow, snow
Glow!

Clouds, answer me this twisted question
Why won't you snow, make me glow?
Make the stars sparkle at night with shepherds' delight
Make the sky in the morning
White like the moon at night . . .
Make it snow, snow
Glow!

Kirsten Leeming (13)
Daventry William Parker School

CAR ATTACK

On last year's Hallowe'en,
A car hit Auntie Jean
Unhinged by this attack
My auntie hit it back.

She hit it with her handbag
And knocked it with her knee
She socked it with a sandbag
And thumped it with a tree.

On last year's Hallow'en
A car hit Auntie Jean
And now, my auntie's better
But the car is with the wrecker.

Leanne Moule (14)
Daventry William Parker School

MY BEST FRIEND

My best friend is
Tall and small
Old and young
Fat and skinny

My best friend has
Blonde and brown hair
Blue and green eyes
Dark and light skin

My best friend is
Funny, clever,
Stupid, dim,
Enthusiastic, humorous,
Sad and happy

My best friend is
Fast and slow
Lazy and helpful
Mature and immature

I don't have one best friend
I have lots.

Daniel Richard Clarke (12)
Daventry William Parker School

FLOWERS

Flowers . . .
They could symbolise grief or bring you elation
But flowers can be used for almost any occasion
So many colours . . . each flower is unique
You could buy a flower for every day of the week.

A bride dressed in white, I guess, would look OK
But that same bride would look fantastic holding a bouquet
It's nice to have a garden with lots of green grass
But a garden with flowers looks better as I pass.

Flowers hang in baskets - suspended on a hook
To preserve some flowers, people press them in a book
They symbolise us well because they, too, can die
Some have a value that even money cannot buy.

Be it a memory or an upcoming event
Flowers are essential - 100 percent
So go on, be daring . . . demonstrate their power.
Go up to someone - and present them with a flower!

Nisha Nalin Patel (12)
Daventry William Parker School

THERE WAS A BOY WHO FELL DOWN A MINE

There was a boy who fell down a mine,
He never knew, there was no sign.
A rock on his head and in despair,
Nobody around to see him there.

At eight years old he died in pain,
Blood and sweat where he had lain,
At the bottom, cold and dark,
When his life had gone, it left no spark!

Emma Goodridge (13)
Daventry William Parker School

THE DAWN OF CHRISTMAS

Excitement rushing through the air,
children's minds go wild.

Santa landing on the roof
trying not to wake the child,
popping down the chimney,
eating all the pies.

Just before he goes,
he leaves the presents behind,
creak, goes the door,
a child peeping through,
Santa spots him there.
With a smile and a wink,
he disappears in a blink.

The child stands there in amazement,
wondering what he has got,
he goes to the presents
and opens, the lot!

Tommy Rice (13)
Daventry William Parker School

MY DOG HARLEY

My dog Harley is like a cuddly bear
he is sometimes mental
he is really friendly
and always sleeping.

My dog Harley is really noisy
he gets really jealous
he is really funny
and always sleeping on my bed.

Always daydreaming
nearly happy every day
really caring every day
he always plays.

He is really smooth
like candyfloss
every time he goes out he
comes in really muddy
he always tosses about.

Laura Smith (12)
Daventry William Parker School

GHOSTS

One dark night I was trembling in my bed,
I was shaking with goosebumps all down my spine.
The rain was dripping down the window,
I peered at my clock, it was ten-past nine.

I could hear the trickling of water from the tap
And the creaking of something on the stairs,
My door slowly opened as the room lit up
And guess who walked in and hid behind the chair?

It was clear, gleaming
And glistening in the night.
It sparkled in silence,
Like a night lamp flickering bright.

Lauren Cugini (12)
Daventry William Parker School

TEENAGE YEARS

Teenage years
are going to be tough -
Trying hard to cope,
school's getting rough.

Lots of people
depending on you,
hard responsibility
everything seems new.

Starting puberty
stomach cramp pain.
Teachers having a go at you
feel like you're going insane.

Little brothers and sisters
getting in your way
but then Mum comes along
to save the day.

She sits down with you
and has a little chat
god, you feel better after that!
You feel like you've got the answer
to a really hard sum.

Take my advice, talk to your mum.

Kimberley Gough (11)
Daventry William Parker School

AUTUMN LIFE

Summer lies beneath heaps of frost,
A blanket of toasted leaves lie on the murky ground,
Whilst crisp conkers spill upon the pavements.

Crimson fireworks splinter the sky,
Rising like fiery flowers then fall into burning showers.
Chipped logs crackle into flames and burn the air
The smoke stains my hair and makes it wispy.

Grey and white clouds gather together
And move swiftly over the misty hillsides.
Then they sprinkle frost, spreading it far and wide,
Freezing the freshly cut lawns.
Then my smoky breath creates a white blur of smoke
Which fills a space in front of me.

A fresh smell of bacon invades my nostrils causing a chill up my spine
As I glide through a basket of soft, scented poppies.
This is the autumn life I live.

Emily Barton (12)
Daventry William Parker School

HOW I HATE WINTER

The short days, the long nights
The cold weather
It's always frosty and icy
How I hate winter.

It looks nice when it snows,
Like a blanket of white
But it is still always cold.
How I hate winter.

How I hate slipping over on the ice
It is invisible like a ghost
When you fall, the coldness makes you numb
How I hate winter.

Nick Thresher (14)
Daventry William Parker School

THE RACE

As we pulled around the corner
Everything was set
We were all ready although very wet.
The starter pushed to green
We were racing at last
Round the first corner
I overtook the first quarter.
Around the second corner
My inspiration took me further.
Up the tall hill
I felt a sudden chill.
Racing up further
My enemy was getting nearer.
Just around the hairpin
It was really hair-raising.
Round the last corner
'First' was in my sight.
It was me and him
This was the greatest fight
I pulled up beside him
And we drew across the line!

Darrell Melotti (12)
Daventry William Parker School

I WISH . . .

I wish I was a somebody
I wish people could see
The kindness of a person
That lives inside of me.

I wish I could fly away
I wish I could be free
As free as a bird
As free as anyone can be.

I wish I was a flower
I wish I sparkled all day
Like a star in the sky
Floating round all day.

I wish I could be the one that people love the most
But when they walk past me, it's as if I'm a ghost
If only I could be the person that's inside me
But that's the only thing that I can't seem to see.

But if I open my eyes
Then I might realise
I should be me
Because that's who I want to be.

Kelly Harvey (12)
Daventry William Parker School

GHOSTS

They're really, really scary
And terrifyingly old
They drift round in the cold
And might be a little hairy.

They drift round and round a tree
And love to scare you out of your skin
Baring their ugly knees
And they can always get in.

Hannah Cheyette (11)
Daventry William Parker School

THE BATTLE OF THE WIND AND THE LEAVES

In the dark of the night,
The wind began to sing.
Then the leaves jumped up
And entered the ring.

The wind gushed about
And gave the leaves a fright.
But the leaves were brave
And prepared for a fight.

Swirling, swerving, soaring in the sky,
The wind, icy cold brought the leaves up high.
Curling, crunching, climbing all around,
The leaves were wounded, but had stood their ground.

Later that night,
The wind died down.
The leaves slowly fell
Back down to the ground.
Now from that night,
The wind wears the gown
But the leaves are the ones,
Which will always be renowned.

Claire Stewart (13)
Daventry William Parker School

MY POEM

My poem's about a castle,
A castle which is big,
My poem's about a hole,
A hole which I've got to dig.

My poem's about my dreams,
My dreams with only me.
My dreams which are private,
Private as can be.

My poem's about me,
Me and my family.
My poem's about a seed,
A seed which will sprout to a tree.

I'm the seed,
I've got to dig the hole,
This is my life,
In my imagination,
I want the castle,
In my dreams,
It's all up to me!

Sophie Harris (12)
Daventry William Parker School

BIRD IN THE SKY

There's a bird in the sky,
Flying low, flying high,
How I'd love to be a bird,
I would fly around the world.

If I could fly, I'd fly to Spain,
Where they don't have much rain,
Up in the treetops I would sing,
Why, oh why can't I have wings?

In winter I wouldn't feel cold,
The feathers keep them warm I'm told,
In the morning birds' singing I heard,
Oh I wish I was a bird.

Emily Skirth (12)
Daventry William Parker School

MAN U

Toot! The second half starts.
Barthez takes a wonderful goal kick!
It goes to Giggs,
He starts his tricks,
He takes his pick,
He goes for . . .

        Goal! 1-0 to Man U!

The game restarts,
It goes to Beckham,
He crosses it in.
Comes off the head of van Nistelrooy
It goes in!
This must be a win!

        Goal! 2-0 to Man U!

Then it's a foul, free kick 20 yards out.
Beckham steps up. It's a *ggoooaaalll!*

Toot! Full-time.

It's a win for Man U!
To take home the FA Cup!

Ben Stewart (11)
Daventry William Parker School

RED

Red is the sunset
Red is a rose
Red is for danger
Red is a cold nose
Red is an autumn leaf
At the summer close.

Red is for ruby
Red is for wine
Red is for valentines
Red is for, 'Will you be mine?'
Red is for *stop*
Or get chased by a cop!

Red is for Ferrari
Red is for cherries
Red is for postbox
Red is for summer berries
Red is for Hell
Where devils dwell.

Red is for strawberries
Red is for lips
Red is for blood
Red is for cold fingertips
Red is for the heart
'Till death us do part!'

Christie Martin (13)
Daventry William Parker School

THE CAT

The cat is a prowler of the night
Its amber eyes are shiny and bright
It walks alone awaiting the light
To watch the birds take-off into flight.

It sits all alone on a wall all day
To watch the children laugh and play
And peaceful and still it will lay
Until the sunshine fades away.

Holly James (12)
Daventry William Parker School

AT LAST IN CHARGE

I walked into the room
Like a timid mouse,
I could see the chairs
Standing to attention,
Waiting for the order,
'Stand at ease.'
Then I could hear a
Series of sounds like
Shotguns coming towards me.
It was boots thumping on the
Hard, shiny, wooden floor.
There were voices shouting, 'Left,
Right, left, right, left, right, left,
Left, left, right, halt.'
They waited for me, they
Glared at me like they
Were about to hit me,
I opened my mouth
And said, 'Sit.'
They all stamped into their
Seats like a herd of elephants.
At last it was
Me in charge.

Scott Hendren (13)
Daventry William Parker School

ALL ALONE

You're all alone in a house
A haunted house I should think

With ghosts and ghouls
And spooks that creep at night

You're all alone in a house
A haunted house I should think

You hear noises, rusty chains rattle
Someone screams, something shrieks

You're all alone in a house
A haunted house I should think

Floorboards creak, doors squeak
Someone's coming. Who is it?

You're all alone in a house
A haunted house I should think

It's getting closer, closer, even closer
You try to hide

You're all alone in a house
A haunted house I should think

You see a cupboard
You run inside

You're all alone in a house
A haunted house I should think

You feel something breathing gently down your neck
You go to look

You're all alone in a house
A haunted house I should think

A pair of fluorescent eyes
You run outside and never go back!

Yasmin Hucknall (12)
Daventry William Parker School

A WORLD OF DARKNESS

Pitch-black, sinister, eerie,
A dark, endless world,
Not a droplet of light around,
The darkness surrounds you
And swallows you up whole,
A bad evil world
Of suffering and pain,
A spooky and secretive world!

Scary, frightening, visionless,
Secretive and sad,
A world of spite and misery,
A hole in the universe,
A black wilderness of shadows,
A never-ending misery,
A spine-chilling, moonless night.

But then it's gone,
Dawn is upon us
And the night has disappeared,
Light beams down on us from above
And darkness spits us out
Until tomorrow.

Megan Smith (12)
Daventry William Parker School

THE HOUSE OF HORROR

I was sleeping heavily
Until I heard a sound,
The sound creaked,
The sound clattered,
I was sitting in my bed, sinking into it,
Hiding under the covers
Shaking with fear.

I decided to go and take a look
To see what was there,
Maybe something terrifying
To really make me scared.

I crept slowly, still shaking,
The noise carried on.
The walls were hissing,
It was pitch-black.
It sounded like I was surrounded
By animals waiting to eat me.
As I crawled down the stairs
The noise got louder and *louder!*
It felt like my skin was ripping off me.

I tripped over my teddy and fell downstairs,
But I was fine.
I walked over to the kitchen
While a cold shiver ran down my spine.
The saucepans rattled,
The window kept opening and shutting.
I ran into the living room
Where I thought it was safe and warm.

It was then silent.
A noise came from the couch.
It said, *'I'm going to kill you.'*
I screamed but nothing came out.
The creature had red eyes
Like a hawk waiting for its prey!
Its fangs fell over its chin.

It walked towards me.
I clenched my teddy and kept my eyes shut.
I screamed but then all I saw was my mum and dad, worried.
We don't live in that house anymore.
I wonder who puts up with the same thing!

Natalie Pow (11)
Daventry William Parker School

SCHOOL

Why do we go to school?
I mean, it's far from cool.
What do you do
Apart from teachers that shout at you?
We go there to learn,
But maths, science, English is not my concern.
You stay there every day for six hours on end
It's enough to drive you round the bend.
Then finally the home time bell,
That's enough of that Hell.

Lucy Murrell (13)
Daventry William Parker School

WINTER

Autumn is ending turning into winter,
The weather is changing from cold to more bitter.
The sheaves of golden leaves have stopped falling
And something is coming, creeping and crawling.

It's come at last and children are out playing,
With gloves on their hands and red cheeks on their faces.
They're building up snowmen and throwing snowballs,
Hoping that more snow will start to fall.

The gardens and trees look like a winter wonderland
With everyone waiting for the trip that's been planned
For it was the night before Christmas with lights and snow
Sleigh bells ringing and Christmas tree lights that glow.

Christmas is here with presents under the tree
Children's faces filled with glee.
Winter is ending, spring draws near
Brings sunshine, flowers and days full of cheer.

Sophie Osborne (12)
Daventry William Parker School

THE DOLPHIN

Dolphin, dolphin in the sea,
How I'd love to be like thee,
Elegant, smart, golden heart,
Glides through the water like a dart.

She is an element in herself,
She needs not friendship, love or wealth,
Glides through the water with golden wings,
Echoes, howls, chimes and sings.

Queen of the oceans, king of the seas,
I beg of you won't you please
Let me have all these things
Especially those golden wings.

Colette Griffin (12)
Daventry William Parker School

IT

It bugs me twenty-four-seven,
Seven to nine, nine till eleven,
It seems like it doesn't leave me alone.

Every time it sees me
You can see stars in its eyes,
It wants to play with me all the time.

Maybe I should move away from my house
In the middle of the night as quiet as a mouse,
But it's still no use it would catch me in a flash
And it would probably eat my cash.
(Then his head with a sponge I'd bash).

I guess I'll have to wait
Till I am not its piece of bait,
That will be another year or two,
Oh what am I going to do?

Oh no, oh no, oh no,
Someone please help me take it away.
Oh it's his seventh birthday and he's left me.

Thank goodness he's older,
My really annoying little brother.

Amy Dennett (12)
Daventry William Parker School

FEAR

A gloomy night,
Shadowy,
The stars were covered with mist
As if they were tucked up in bed.
A silhouette,
A silhouette was following me.
A chill down my spine like it was blowing at me.
The wind, or so I thought, sounded like a ghost
Chasing me, hounding me down the pavement.
It breezed past, I gasped.
I inhaled the cold, wet, damp air,
I exhaled my fear into it.
It almost touched me,
I ran,
It followed.
Its dark black figure, one foot at a time,
Slowly catching up with me.
I ran faster and faster,
Like a bad dream I couldn't escape.
The road seemed endless.
Eventually a stream of orange, red and yellow
Appearing on the horizon.
Glorious light, shining light, rays of light,
I turned, it had disappeared, back to the dark, to nowhere.
My heart, my pulsating heart had dropped.

Joseph Ashwell (11)
Daventry William Parker School

HALLOWE'EN IS THE NIGHT!

Boo!
He jumped out at me like a lion.
Scary costume.
I'm as white as a ghost.

I love trick or treat.
Masks are scary.
Dark,
As dark as dust.

Tammy Smith (14)
Daventry William Parker School

HAMSTERS

Hamsters are really small
Running around in their exercise ball
Crash and bash but never fall
Really furry and pretty cool.

Nathaniel Carter (12)
Daventry William Parker School

GHOSTS

Lying in my bed, cosy and warm,
There is a new ghost being born.
A ghost in a tin can
Scared of man
I pray tonight he will not form.

Lying in my bed, cosy and warm,
It's weeping and creeping but I'm cosy and warm,
The dark night is white, it's now out of sight,
Goodnight.
Sleep tight.

Sam Parry-Howard (11)
Daventry William Parker School

SECRET HAVEN

Bluey-green water cascading down the hillside
Into a hot mist of foam,
Over some sharp, jagged rocks
And around a bend the little brook
Comes to its end.
I walk away from this every day
Hoping that no one will find it hidden away,
It's a secret haven.

Claire Draisey (14)
Daventry William Parker School

THE FOUNTAIN

The fountain is amazing
Providing water cascading.

The colours are changing,
It's quite amazing.

It's started to slow,
There's no colour surrounding.

Liam Pickard (14)
Daventry William Parker School

NIGHT-TIME

In the dark and shining blue sky
The moon is sparkling brightly,
The rain is hitting the windowpane,
The stars make the sky look splendid.

The orbit around the fantastical Earth
Which makes me feel so happy,
I see rockets shooting high
Into the dark, dazzling night.

Louise Gibbons (12)
Daventry William Parker School

WATER

Water,
A waterfall of white water,
The sea full of salt,
A little stream trickles by
Into a sparkling river,
Through a misty mountain,
Under a bridge of stone
Into a sparkling ocean.

Chris Atkins (13)
Daventry William Parker School

THE SEA

The sea,
Glistening moonlight on ripples of water,
Waves splashing gently against the shore,
Twisting, turning,
White horses running,
Seaweed sparkling
In the deep blue sea.

Samantha Rogers (13)
Daventry William Parker School

EYE SPY . . .

I spy a dragon pink and green,
I spy a dragon never before seen,
I spy a dragon big and bold,
I spy a dragon wise and old,
I spy a dragon in the clouds,
I spy a dragon so very loud.
I spy a dragon in my dreams,
I spy a dragon, I scream and scream,
I spy . . . a dragon.

Nicole Reid (12)
Daventry William Parker School

WATER SHOW

Water explodes as a spray of mist,
A torrent of pouring water,
Gathering water as clear as glass,
A spout of water creates a swell of white horses,
The fountain provides an amazing water show.

James Taylor (14)
Daventry William Parker School

THE MAN ON THE MOON!

The man on the moon lives with the sparkling stars,
He climbs in the craters on Venus and Mars.

In the winter on Earth it rains quite happily
But on the planet Neptune the weather is higgledy-piggledy.

When the people on Earth have contests with beauty,
An eclipse on the moon is the moon man's duty.

But when the sun comes in the morning sky
The moon and the stars fade fantastically by!

Nicol Gray (12)
Daventry William Parker School

A SAD SPACEMAN

A man on the moon,
A sparkling star,
A curve shape,
Twisting nonsense of space,
Back to Earth,
A sad man
Missing his orbit.

Alexander Hutchinson (12)
Daventry William Parker School

CHILDREN

C   is for children being all alone.
H   is for horrid when they're beat to the bone.
I   is for idol, not really caring.
L   is for lonely and always swearing.
D   is for disabled and feeling mad.
R   is for revenge that you never had.
E   is for example for you to follow.
N   is for nasty and full of sorrow.

Suzanne Taylor (13)
Daventry William Parker School

THE WINTRY NIGHT

The sun goes down at three
and the children go home from school
to be cosy and warm in their homes,

It goes dark and gloomy, the moon comes up
and brightens up the midnight sky.
The stars come out to join the moon
and make the sky pretty and blue.
To make the night really perfect,
snow slowly floats down to the ground.

The night has ended and the sun comes up,
the moon goes down to wait for another
night to shine as bright.

Becky Minns (14)
Daventry William Parker School

THE WEIRD POEM

Hot cocoa on chilly nights,
Children cuddling up with no frights,
The wind twists and curves and blows the snow
And people's cheeks go cold and glow.

Then I wonder, is this a load of nonsense
Me trying to write an assonance?
I've been told to write what I want to say,
About what I think of every day.

I've been writing this poem for half an hour,
It's a lot harder than working a shower.

Carly Jackson (14)
Daventry William Parker School

SNOW

Snow falls in the winter season,
It is soft, white and extremely freezing.
People pick it up and make it into balls,
When they play they don't stick to the rules.

People make bases of snow and play war
And when they're gone they just make some more.
People lie down and make angels on the ground,
Children shout and make a horrendous sound.

Snow is a fun game, full of shouting.
Snowballs flying around, hitting and clouting.
Snow comes, made in all shapes and sizes.
Christmas is a time for family and is full of
                              prezzies and surprises.

Merry Christmas everyone.

Vicky Boikovs
Daventry William Parker School

TWISTED

There was a twisted street
and in the twisted street there was a twisted house
and in the twisted house there was a twisted room
and in the twisted room there was a twisted mouse.

Above the twisted house there was a twisted moon
and a twisted sky that twisted even more at noon.

And the twisted stars were twisting to the sky
but as the sun came up, they began to die.

Jodie Mandefield (13)
Daventry William Parker School

AIR RAID

Hitler's bombs are screaming down
Heading straight for London town.
But Churchill's planes are drawing near
Blowing the swastika down back to Hell.

All destruction, all fear,
Those Nazi swine drink women's tears.

Down in the shelters, that musty air
Coughing and choking but spirits are high,
High as the birds soaring in the sky.
Hitler hasn't achieved his end
Churchill will send his army great
Right into the hearts of evil men.

England will fight, fight to the end,
We will never give up!

Our country will rise, rise to victory,
Hitler can't penetrate our determination.

Steven Tompkins (13)
Daventry William Parker School

THE RAINBOW

I watch the rain run down the window
And I can see a bit of a rainbow,
There's red, orange, yellow and green,
They are all beginning to lean
As the sun begins to show.

Louise Brown (11)
Daventry William Parker School

THE SUN

The burning thing in orbit,
The one and only star,
It sparkles in the dark
And reaches ever so far.

People haven't been there,
As you would burn to death,
It's hotter than you can imagine,
So don't bother booking a trip there.

It brings us light,
It brings us heat,
What more can you ask?

Luke Jones (13)
Daventry William Parker School

DRIVING

I am driving a racing car
Racing down the street
I swerve round the bend
And that is the end
Of my own pride and joy.

Oh my Subaru Impreza
I've had a lot of lecture
Off my mechanic friends
It's battered and rammed
Like a flat pan
Oh why does this have to happen?

Rajen Jayantilal Mistry (11)
Daventry William Parker School

WHY DO I HAVE TO BE A BABY?

Why do I have to be a baby?
All I can do is be lazy!
I wish I could be happy,
They even make me wear this stupid nappy!

I want to go outside and play in the snow,
Not just lie here and watch it glow!

They must think I'm so dumb,
I can wipe my own bum!
I want to kick my mum and dad,
Then maybe it wouldn't be so bad!

One day I'll dress myself

And then I'll buy a car!

Ga, ga, ga!

Holly Jelley (14)
Daventry William Parker School

A RAINBOW OF TEENAGE EMOTIONS

Red is the frustration that burns inside.
Orange is the embarrassment that makes you run and hide.
Yellow is the 'Hello!' of a cheerful morning.
Green is the content of not being in mourning.
Blue is misery for the down and depressed.
Indigo is the doubt that hangs in my chest.
Violet is devotion for one in love.
My coloured emotions are shown up above.

Jacob Szikora (13)
Daventry William Parker School

WHAT WAS IT?

Tall and big
Wide and fat
Great big feet
Chunky and flat
Spiky back
Humpy too
What is it?
Please give me a clue.
The neck is long
Its tail is too
The teeth are sharp
And it's looking at you.
I smell burning
Look up there
I think there're flames appearing in the air!
Its nostrils are flaring, getting rather round.
'Quick let's get out of here
But don't make a sound!'

Sean Joshua Smith (13)
Daventry William Parker School

SKATERS

Skaters
Skate, tricky
Cool, dangerous, painful,
Skaters perform well
Skaters.

Adam Bradley (13)
Daventry William Parker School

CHRISTMAS TIME

Kids are decorating the big green tree,
hanging up stockings by the fire
in hope that Santa Claus will fill them with
presents like sweets and toys.

Then when Christmas Eve is here
kids are so excited they don't want to sleep,
so parents say, 'Go to bed or Santa Claus
won't give you presents.'
So upstairs the kids go and fall straight asleep.

The very next morning the kids go downstairs
and can't believe their eyes when they look at
the bulging stockings and the tree with presents
surrounding the bottom.
They start ripping off the wrapping paper to
find . . . wonderful . . . toys!

Christy Louden (11)
Daventry William Parker School

ALL ALONE

She walked through valleys of shadows
as deep as darkness at night.
She stumbled upon a forest
with a leafy, golden floor.
Then fiery flames grew all around her
imprisoning her in a cage of heat.
She broke free and screamed a
deafening ear-piercing scream
which shook the moonlit night.

Antonia Brown (11)
Daventry William Parker School

I LOVE CHRISTMAS

I really love Christmas,
It makes me feel so happy,
I don't care if it's raining,
The stars are sparkling,
It makes me feel great.

I love the beauty of Christmas,
Everything is so colourful,
Even the boring people twist and curve,
In a higgledy-piggledy way,
And when it's dark,
The moon orbits us and makes it so bright.

All these things make me . . .
Love Christmas.

Alex Bunn (12)
Daventry William Parker School

FIREWORKS

Fireworks are bright,
They sparkle in the night.

Fireworks swirl,
Fireworks curl.

Fireworks prancing,
Fireworks dancing.

Fireworks falling slowly
                    to the ground.

Cheryl Beacham (11) & Layla Reid (12)
Daventry William Parker School

MERRY CHRISTMAS!

Hannah's waiting in the snow,
She wonders when her friends will show.
But Frankie's rushing round a shop
She needs a special Christmas top.

And Aaron's dancing to a new CD,
Oh no! He's fallen! He hits the tree
Which falls onto Jay, who's feeling perky,
Guess who's eaten all the turkey?

There's Calvin with the mistletoe,
Watch out girls, you never know!
And Daisy's wishing on a star,
That Santa Claus is not too far.

Rochelle remembers Hannah's waiting
And calls the others, anticipating
The greatest party, but someone's missing!
Here comes Stacy and she's wishing . . .

A merry Christmas to everyone,
We all hope you have lots of fun!

Jenelle Burgess (12)
Daventry William Parker School

MY FRIENDS

My friends are cool, as cool as can be
They're very nearly as cool as me!
I like my friends, we have a laugh
We always hang out along the path.

Jenny Jenkins (11)
Daventry William Parker School

CHRISTMAS DAY

Christmas Day is getting near
I cannot wait till it's here
The Christmas tree stands proud and tall
The best thing though is no more school, yes!
All the gifts, big and bright
Sitting under the Christmas lights.
We share Christmas with family and friends
Their love for Christmas they like to send.
The doorbell goes, *ding, dong, ding*!
It's the carollers and they've come to sing.
The snow and the cold don't get in the way
Of our wonderful, brilliant Christmas Day.
We settle down to a nice mince pie
Then Christmas goes, oh bye-bye!

Bianca Bewley (13)
Daventry William Parker School

STORM

No scream of the sun,
No howling of the wind,
You can hear the thunder,
Crackles of the downpour,
Splashes and squalls
And blow and roar,
Rustling and whistling,
As you hear the trickling into puddles,
Sun - everywhere,
It shines its light.

Melissa Hunt (11)
Daventry William Parker School

MONSTER TIME

I jump up, what was that?
It could be Fluffy, my cat
Something is on my bed,
'I'll kill you,' is what it said
I fall and scream
Hoping it is just a dream
But no, it is there, sitting on the floor
I run downstairs to find there are more
They come towards me, daggers in hands
I sink to the floor like I'm in quicksand
I am now trapped in their little game
This is starting to be a pain
The monster starts to make me shudder
I scream out loud for my mother
The morning sun rises
The monster dies
I climb up, everyone is still in bed
And there on the floor, Fluffy is dead.

Marie Newberry (11)
Daventry William Parker School

CHRISTMAS DAY

Christmas Day is merry, it's a time for giving,
It's a very happy time of the year,
The people are very cheerful and heart-warming,
People have lots of presents on Christmas Day!

Ho! Ho! Ho!
Merry Christmas!

Ryan White (12)
Daventry William Parker School

WATER

Water splashes all around
up onto the cliffs
salty water, crashing sound
sea waves rise and fall.

'Water, water everywhere'
what a famous saying
water mixed with hair dye
to stop the age of greying.

Water travels round the world
with tiny bits of gold
crashed against the sand and hurled
water . . . so strange.

Declan Jerimiah Dudley (11)
Daventry William Parker School

THE ROCKET

As you light a rocket,
It goes up, up and up into the sky,
Then it makes a big bang and explodes.

It all shoots out in different directions.
It has bright colours,
Reds, yellows, browns, greens and lots more
Wonderful colours.

As it comes down, it crackles
And all the debris scatters for miles
And lands on the ground with a thud.

Richard Cooper (11)
Daventry William Parker School

NEW YEAR

10, 9, 8, almost time
7, 6, 5, 4, I can't wait
3, 2, 1, at last, a whole new year!

Crack, bang, whizz, the fireworks are off,
                     they are wicked
It's midnight on 2003,
I can't wait for next year.

It's so loud, I've got a headache,
Screaming and whistling like mad,
I can't hear anything.

My New Year's resolution is,
to eat as much chocolate as possible,
better not tell Mum and Dad.

When I get home I wonder if
this year will be the same as last
or if it'll be different, let's just see!

Andrew Proffitt (11)
Daventry William Parker School

WINTER BEACH

Oceans, calm, quiet, silent, soft,
White snowflakes fall to the sand that glitters,
Jagged rocks as smooth as silk,
Wind, graceful and silent,
Oceans, calm, quiet, silent, soft.

Emily Evans (13)
Daventry William Parker School

THE CAVE'S SECRET

In a dark, gloomy forest
A grim cave lies,
Something dwells within it,
With emerald-green eyes.

Its body is a mystery,
Its never been seen,
But those who have seen his head,
Say he's evil and mean.

He has sharp, jagged teeth
And wicked, pointy ears,
He is the creature
That everyone fears.

His nostrils flare to smell you,
If you step near his lair,
Escaping from this monster
Is extremely rare.

You can hear his frightful groaning,
From miles around
It is a really scary,
Petrifying sound.

Does he whine because he's hungry?
Does he ever stop groaning?
Does he cry because he's happy?
Or maybe he's just lonely?

Emma Dyer (13)
Daventry William Parker School

ON THE AFRICAN SAVANNAH

Sitting on the balcony
I hear elephants trumpeting,
Lions roaring,
Crickets chirping on the African savannah.

Walking through the grass,
Gazelles jumping in a big pack,
Meerkats standing to attention,
Warthogs shuffling on the African savannah.

Soon the day was over,
The sun sank beneath the clouds,
I can taste the atmosphere,
I can smell the life on the African savannah.

Rebecca Proffitt (13)
Daventry William Parker School

SNOW

Snow,
Flaky snow falling down,
Slippy ice under your feet,
Snow crunching as you walk along the path,
Flakes falling on your head,
Ice crystals falling off the roofs of houses above,
Avalanche crashing down the mountains,
Magical sounds as the snow falls down.

Rosie Cave (14)
Daventry William Parker School

THE POLTERGEIST

Falling flowlessly to the ground,
Smashing in my face,
As the objects around me disappeared,
With pieces in their place.

I turned to the kitchen door,
As the door hinges creaked,
As the cupboard door opened,
The glasses in them shattered
One, two, three,
Then the rest.

The garden door opened,
And put the smashing to rest!

James Renouf (11)
Daventry William Parker School

ALL ON MY OWN

The night wind rattles the window frame
I wake up shivering, shivering all alone.
Darkness, silence. What's the time?
Mother's asleep and Dad's not home.
Shivering in the corner, shivering all alone.

Who's there - standing behind the curtain?
Shivering in the corner, no need to cry . . .
It's only the shadow of the tree in the garden.
Shaking and sighing as the wind rushes by,
Shivering in the corner and no need to cry.

And then I was all on my own!

Ethan Roberts (12)
Daventry William Parker School

I'M WISHING FOR A WHITE CHRISTMAS

Stars bright, moon so bright,
Everyone's sleeping so silently tonight.
It's nearly Christmas and everyone's playing
Children are giggling and saying,
'Hip hip hooray, joy to all today.'
It's Christmas Eve today
And everyone wants a white Christmas,
Santa comes, sprinkles his magic.
The children wake, the snow falls down
Snowmen are made all around the town
Everyone's happy, they've got what they wanted
A white Christmas
Hip, hip hooray!

Anna Brinklow (12)
Daventry William Parker School

FOOTBALL!

Ryan Giggs doing his tricks
Roy Keane gives 'im a kick.
David Becks on the edge of the box
Oh my god, his shot bloomin' rox.
Mikael Silvestre bootin' it out
One of the fans gives 'im a shout.
Nicky Butt being tripped up
One of the opposition givin' a tut.
David Becks outside the box again
He curves it well, oh how it bends.
Man United coming out victors
All of their fans are mad addictors.

Sam Haynes (11)
Daventry William Parker School

WINTER WEATHER

The nights are drawing in.
The lightness is getting dim.
The weather is colder
As the days are getting older.
The leaves are being pulled off the trees
By that cold, dark winter breeze.
Animals are getting ready to sleep
Some are burrowing in homes really deep.
Birds are flying to hotter places
As you see them, they look as if they're in races.
People are wrapping up warmly in their winter clothes
Because again winter's waiting outside your door
Everywhere you turn winter has come again.

Alana Palin (12)
Daventry William Parker School

FORMULA 1

1 red light and screens down
2 red lights and feet on rests
3 red lights and engines on
4 red lights and hands on wheels
5 red lights and turns to green
Go, go, go!
Round the corner at 200mph
Racing towards the post
The chequered flag is in the air
David Coulthard pulls in front
The Scot wins the race.
Winner!

Tom Souter (11)
Daventry William Parker School

WAR

Greed and anger leads to war
Starting with rich countries fighting the poor.

Thousands of soldiers going to fight
People dying all through the night.

Blood, terror, bullets and guns
Body parts flying like liver and lungs.

Soldiers wounded and screaming for help
Life flashing before them as memories melt.

Families worried as people will die
Not knowing what's happened so start to cry.

Power is near as they have nearly won
When they thought it was over, it has only begun . . .

Nick Berry (12)
Daventry William Parker School

YELLOW

Yellow are the stars out of our reach,
Yellow is the sand on a tropical beach.
Yellow is the colour of the blazing sun,
Yellow is the icing on a hot sticky bun.
Yellow is the sky at the sunrise hour,
Yellow is the petal of a bright sunflower.
Yellow is the colour of an autumn leaf,
Yellow is the colour of a coral reef.
Yellow can be the pattern on a butterfly's wings,
Yes - yellow is many things.

Nadia Chem (12)
Daventry William Parker School

FREAKY HOUSE!

In a crooked house at night,
A light turned on ever so bright.

Suddenly there was a creak on the floor,
A bash on the door
And footsteps coming towards me!

I crawled up into a ball
And wished I was at school.

It whispered in my ear,
'There's no need to fear!'

A sudden chill filled the air
I turned to look
But nothing was there!

Sarah Pancoust (12)
Daventry William Parker School

MY BEST FRIEND

My best friend's name is Nelly
Her real name is Jenelle
She's independent, kind and merry
She's brave and determined as well.

She's gentle, giving, mature and brave
And she never goes off in a demanding rage
She's sensible, sociable, strong and cool
Although she sometimes acts like a fool.

That's my best friend, Nelly.

Charlotte Dickinson (12)
Daventry William Parker School

THE SCARY NIGHT

As I lay in my bed on that scary night
My body shivered and my back went cold,
Someone was out there ready to get me.
All the noises outside made me lie in my bed still, quiet,
I didn't make a noise.
I heard a bang coming from downstairs,
I lay awake still quite cold!
Footsteps I heard were coming faster and faster,
I laid stiller and stiller.
The door opened with a creak,
I saw something,
It had red shining eyes.
I screamed louder and louder,
The door slammed shut.
Then I just lay still, cold,
Awake on that scary night.
Will it come again?

Amy James (12)
Daventry William Parker School

RAIN

I stare out my window and I see
Rain coming down, as fast as can be,
Gently patting my windowpane,
English weather, it's always the same.
Puddles forming on the ground
All is quiet, no one's around,
Slowly dripping, now there's almost none,
Going, going, going, gone.

Aimée Best (13)
Daventry William Parker School

A HAIR-RAISING NIGHT

On a cold winter's night,
A man got a fright,
Walking down a path.

He saw three ghosts,
All sitting on posts
And eating mice and rats.

They all said, *'Boo!'*
Made a hullabaloo,
The man was scared stiff.

He ran and ran,
Did that man,
Back down the ghostly path.

But from that night,
With fright,
His hair went completely . . . white!

Camille Davies (11)
Daventry William Parker School

DOLPHINS

D   olphins are . . .
O   riginal
L   ovely
P   eaceful
H   appy
I   ntelligent
N   atural
S   mooth.

Simone Smyth (11)
Daventry William Parker School

NOISES THAT SCARE ME

N obody can hear them,
O nly me.
I t comes at night and goes in the morning.
S cary. Oh very scary.
E rnie, my bear, is tight to my chest,
S ooner I wake up the better.

T hat cold and sick voice.
H omeless people are shouting in my head.
A ghost or ghoul or monster is after me
T ight grip of Ernie, my bear.

S hots from cannons,
C urly waves in my head,
A ction, screaming in my head,
R ushing in my brain
E rnis is a bear, but I know he can hear them

M iaow, the cat shrieks,
E rnie on the floor, noises stopped, it's the morning.

Holly Bevan (11)
Daventry William Parker School

CHRISTMAS

It's Christmas Eve
and we all decorate the tree
we all wait till it's late
and try to stay awake
and when we wake, before our eyes
is a bundle of presents
which give us a great surprise.

Sarah Russell (11)
Daventry William Parker School

GHOSTS AND GHOULS COME OUT TONIGHT!

Ghosts and ghouls come out tonight,
They come to haunt your house,
Ghosts and ghouls come out tonight,
To suck your world into Hell.

Ghosts and ghouls play out tonight,
They shriek, scream and shout,
Ghosts and ghouls play out tonight,
They'll smash up all the town.

Ghosts and ghouls hang out tonight,
They make electricity go *bang!*
Ghosts and ghouls hang out tonight,
They lurk in the darkness, on your land.

They're coming to get you!

Gwendoline Ford (12)
Daventry William Parker School

THE BATTLE

The enemy charged over the horizon
sweeping away the defences with ease.
The defenders were rebellious
but the attackers aggressively stormed
the earthwork defences, leaving a trail
of death and destruction behind them.

As the sky and the ground turned a dull blood-red
The victorious army looted and destroyed any
remaining buildings.

Gareth Martin (11)
Daventry William Parker School

CASPER THE GHOST

I'm Casper the ghost,
I really love to scare.
Always hiding here and there,
Jumping out at people and then *roar!*
Ha, ha, ha that made you hide
Behind the door.

I'm Casper the ghost,
I really like the graveyards.
I especially love to jump out
On people at a funeral.
I'm Casper the ghost and
I really love to scare!
Boo!

Georgina Baker (11)
Daventry William Parker School

THE RED DRAGON

Red Dragon howling, hissing, exploding.
The light lights up the sky.
The people are loading.

The firework fizzes and flies high
It screams like a thing from Hell
The people look up and are amazed.

The man leant back so far he fell
He lay on the floor, dazed.

The Red Dragon!

Joshua Holdridge (11)
Daventry William Parker School

SO LITTLE TIME

6am up at dawn,
Rushing to get ready and travel all morn,
So little time.
8am on the plane,
Ready to fly and play my game,
So little time.
10am arrive at Hollywood
To go and see the premier of Robin Hood,
So little time.
2pm finally I have time to hang with
My favourite Daniel Radcliffe,
So little time.
6pm time to have dinner
With my best mate David Schwimmer,
So little time.
10pm time for bed,
'Coz tomorrow I'm hanging with cousin Edd,
So little time.

Heather Maude (12)
Daventry William Parker School

CHRISTMAS

It's Christmas Eve
everyone's decorated the tree
we wait until it's midnight
then we fall fast asleep
we run down the stairs
and into the living room
and before our eyes - presents!

Amy Smalley (12)
Daventry William Parker School

THE SEA

The sea,
Smashing froth,
Waves spray,
Super salty sea.

The sea crushing the sand,
Wind, torrent change,
Undulating waves,
Colossal amount of water.

The sea,
Smashing against boats,
Crushing waves,
The deep blue sea,
The sea.

Joseph Skinner (13)
Daventry William Parker School

THE FIVE KIDS

One late Friday five kids turned up for school
Where are the others?
They're at the pool.

One late Friday five kids turned up for swimming
Where are the others?
Watching football, they're winning.

One late Friday five kids turned up for football
Where are the others?
They're in the hall.

Luke Hickman (11)
Daventry William Parker School

WEST HAM

David James saving a great shot
No wonder he's the best keeper of the lot,
Sebastian Schemmel a great defender
He likes cool clothes, what a great spender.

Tomas Repka, a rough and tough guy
I met him in the street once and he said, 'Hi!'
Christian Dailly, a really big Scotsman
He told me he likes to drink Coke out of a can.

Nigel Winterburn, he's 38 years old
That's why he's getting so bald.
Trevor Sinclair running up the left wing
He crosses and Kanoute made a great swing.

Jermaine Defoe, a little English man
I saw him giving someone a can.
Paulo Di Canio, the greatest forward in the world
He tried to drink a bottle of milk, but it was curdled.

Aaron Kilshaw (11)
Daventry William Parker School

MY DOG DOM

My dog Dom is small and fluffy
He is a Yorkshire terrier puppy
He makes me laugh the way he runs
With my other dog he always has fun
He eats his food like lightning
When he feels ill he's always frightening
People say he's really sweet
But when they come round he acts all neat.

Tamsin Taylor-White (12)
Daventry William Parker School

WINTER

The snow has started falling
And children are shouting and calling
That their favourite time of year has come,
The summer afternoons of play are over and done.

The bare trees stand alone,
In a forest which was once known,
The freezing cold, wet weather is here
And the snow falls to the ground as if it's never been near.

The sun sets early, about 5 o'clock,
When the icy winds blow and the trees will rock,
Christmas is getting closer, about a week to go,
What presents the children will be getting, they do not know.

All the homes around look joyful and festive,
The Christmas trees stand up sparkling and decorative,
Snowballs are flying everywhere because everyone's excited,
Children are acting in Christmas plays and parents are delighted.

Lauren Robinson (12)
Daventry William Parker School

XMAS!

When I wake up in the morning and I run downstairs,
Everyone is just standing there,
Shocked and surprised at how many presents to see,
Let's open them, what can they be?
Stars hanging from the ceiling
Xmas tree, glittering and gleaming.
Xmas is no longer here,
Don't worry though, it will be here next year!

Hollie Unger (12)
Daventry William Parker School

GHOST

I heard a scary noise last night
It gave me quite a fright
I wasn't sure if I was dreaming
So I didn't dare start screaming.

I looked all around
There it was sitting in a mound
I was lying frozen still
I started to make my will.

Then I thought it could be my cat
Or maybe a tiny, old rat
I sat up in my bed
And called out to my cat, 'Ted, Ted!'

Then I decided to turn on the light
I squinted, it was bright
It turned out it was a bat
It was worse than a bite from a gnat.

Charlotte Brander (11)
Daventry William Parker School

DRUMS, DRUMS

Drums, drums in the deep,
We cannot get out,
The doors are locked, but cannot hold them for long.
Drums, drums in the deep,
Deeper and deeper they go into the shadow.
Drums, drums in the shadow,
They are coming . . .

Daniel Clements (11)
Daventry William Parker School

WATER

Water from the sea is calm
When the sun is going down,
But when it's windy
The sea gets rough and creates a wild storm.
When the waves break on the beach
It looks like white horses running up the sand.
We can see marine life jumping around in the waters,
The sea is glistening on the surface of the sea.
As the night falls two misty figures walk along the beach
To watch the sun going down on the horizon
Upon the crooked cliff there is a small hut
Which glistens under the moonlit sky.
Early morning when the rain comes down
The little wooden hut is no longer in sight.

Carron Barnes (13)
Daventry William Parker School

THE DRAGON

The dragon,
Scaly, green and angry,
Mythological, magical creature
Walking around the land,
Breathing fire at anything in its way,
With its long, sharp, pointing tail
It's different to everything else,
Wings that stretch for miles,
Horns as big as men,
Big, long, sharp nails that tear up
The ground as he walks.

Laura Courtney (13)
Daventry William Parker School

THE POLTERGEIST

I was alone, scared. Awake one night,
When I saw an eerie sight.
An object was floating in the air,
But at first I didn't care.
At first I thought I was asleep,
But not for long, out of bed I leaped.
I ran into my parent's room
And told them about the impending doom.
They didn't believe a word I said, they said,
'Get back to bed!'
Every night it happens there,
Why can't it just disappear into thin air?

Christopher Cosentino (11)
Daventry William Parker School

RUGBY!

The ref blows his whistle,
The game's about to start,
The players' hearts are racing,
Their feet pacing around the pitch,
The scrums, the malls,
Ouch, that's got to hurt,
Medics on the pitch.

The ambulance sirens are wailing,
The doctors frown at his broken leg,
He'll be out for six weeks at least.

Sam Brentegani (11)
Daventry William Parker School

BEWARE!

Ghostly houses on sweet town square,
When you walk past them they'll give you a scare.
They'll make you shiver, send a chill down your spine.

Just one look and you'll be scared out of your wits,
You will crumble away into 1000 little bits.

You hear eerie noises,
Crunch, crack, whack, boom,
You wonder what's going on in the gloom.

Floorboards cackling, walls whispering,
These houses are as grim as grim can be
And they're as slimy as a snake.

Step inside if you dare, but I warned you
So *beware!*

Abigail Dawes (11)
Daventry William Parker School

STUNTS

Stunts are cool
They absolutely rule
Stuntmen dare each other
To jump out of the air
They blow up cars
Right up to the stars
Stunts are cool
They absolutely rule!

Daniel Grocott (12)
Daventry William Parker School

CHOCOLATE

Chocolate, chocolate,
Nice and sweet.

Chocolate is so good to eat.

Nice and creamy.
Soft and dreamy.

Eating it without a care,
My brother's says it's so unfair.

It's mine, not yours,
So go away.

Now my chocolate's
Here to stay,

. . . but not for long.

Sally Ronch (13)
Daventry William Parker School

OWLS

Owls take flight,
Moving swiftly through the night.

Swooping down on their prey
As the mouse runs away.

Large yellow eyes,
Looking down as he flies.

Claws as sharp as knives,
Scaring children, men and wives.

Darren Mann (13)
Daventry William Parker School

THE HOUSE OF SCARES

At a haunted house
On a full moon night,
Jeremy Footlong
Was having a fright.
With a wallop and a crack
The ghost hit his head,
Then Jeremy Footlong
Tiptoed to bed.
That night a shiver ran down his spine,
When he heard something creepy downstairs
He ran down with a knife, he never went back,
As it's the terrible house of scares.

Nicholas Kitchen (11)
Daventry William Parker School

ANGER

Anger is like a burning fire
Bubbling away in your heart's desire.
Anger is a roaring devil
Growing up and down your spine.
Anger is like gushes of blood
Scarlet in colour, thick as mud.
Anger is like seizing rage
A devil dancing with his slave.
Anger is a shiny dagger
Sharp in a lash, quick as a flash.
Anger is an uncontrollable thing,
As it lasts just like a fling.

Victoria Statham (13)
Daventry William Parker School

SPORT

The crowd roar as
loud as an aeroplane
taking off.

The ball flies through
the air pushing the
wind aside.

The pitch is like a cage
with fans all around
trapping the players inside.

The ground tastes the
ball as the players
fight their fight.

Daniel Havard (13)
Daventry William Parker School

GHOULS AND GHOSTS

Ghouls and ghosts outside my house,
It can't be that bad,
It might be a mouse.

Cracks and crunches up my path,
Can't they do this later?
Like after my bath.

Squeaks and creaks they're getting closer,
What shall I do?
I know I'll use my toaster.

Nickie Gisdakis (11)
Daventry William Parker School

Nobody Knows Me

Nobody knows me,
Not really,
They just see
The outside of me.

I sit and look
At everyone play
Like a big family
And I'm the odd one out.

I hear them singing
And shouting like a
Big band had
Just appeared.

If only one day
Just once
Someone would come
And play with me.

Natasha Fakih (13)
Daventry William Parker School

Dragons

D   irty dragons
R   ough and cold
A   ngry dragons
G   ruesome and bold
O   bnoxious dragons
N   asty and old.

Hannah Carlill (12)
Daventry William Parker School

Autumn

Animals
Scurry around
The trees
Ready to hibernate.

Rustling
Leaves,
Brown
And red.

Running through
The cold, cold wind,
It whistles through my hair,
Cold like snow.

Bonfires' flames
Go, go, go.

Hannah Davis (13)
Daventry William Parker School

The Ocean

The ocean smells like seaweed,
You can see it for miles.
Green, blue and white waves,
Splashing against the rocks.
It sounds like the wind blowing
Through the trees.
If feels as cold as ice
And it tastes as bitter as salt,
When I trip it engulfs me.

Claire Healey (13)
Daventry William Parker School

THAT WORD

I'm sitting in the room
With the white piece
Of paper which
Lies on the table staring at me.
It's just that word,
The word in big block letters.

The teacher standing there watching me,
The time is nearly up
And I can see the door,
It's telling me to run,
It's telling me to get out.

It's the word, it is like being in a cell
Where shivers run down my spine.
I just can't say the word,
Time is up, I have not finished the
Test.

Heidi McKay (13)
Daventry William Parker School

MY POEM

All alone in the dark,
I shiver in my comfy bed.
The creaking of the staircase,
I go further down in my bed.
The wind howling through the window,
All the shadows I see.
I go down further in my bed,
Closing my eyes tight shut.

Adam Robson (11)
Daventry William Parker School

THE SEASIDE

I love to go to the seaside,
I love to splash about.
I love to dig holes so I can jump in
And then jump out.

The sun is coming out, I am really happy.
Nonsense is the only thing happier,
It starts to rain.
The sun is a searing beauty.
I can see a rainbow in the sky,
It is a lovely colour.

It is getting cold and dark.
I can see sparkling stars up in the sky.
I have to go now
But when I go next year I will tell you all about it.

Roxanne Davis (12)
Daventry William Parker School

BEWARE OF THE HAUNTED HOUSE!

The night wind rattles the window frame
As the door clicks open again,
Upon the garden path the leaves crunch
And just at that time you hear a munch,
You go through the kitchen door
When you hear something smash on the floor,
You turn around to take a look
But guess who's standing there, *beware,*
Beware of the haunted house!

Gemma Berrill (11)
Daventry William Parker School

THE HORSE

The horse's hooves curved in the rain,
The twist and shape of the horse's mane,
The people around natter words of nonsense,
The eyes of the rider sparkling like stars,
The dark horse jumps the fantastical bars,
The rider felt like he was in orbit,
The colours rushed through his head,
The second jump had been conquered,
He noticed a man looking melancholy,
The quietude of the crowd as the bay horse galloped on,
The softer legs shone,
The last jump, the highest bar,
Well done, we've won, well done, Star.

Kirsten Wright (12)
Daventry William Parker School

FAT FOODS

Food I love I simply do
But once you know what you've eaten
It comes back to you.
All the pounds and stones
I used to be near to bones
I feel so ugly and fat
Being an elephant
I've never fancied that
I must have looked like a right pig
I never thought of myself as being that big.

Abbie Thomas (13)
Daventry William Parker School

THE DRAGON

First a peeping eye
From beneath a rock.
Then some snarling lips
Stuck behind a lock.

Then some long sharp claws
Scratching on the ground.
The scaly legs come out
From underneath a mound.

Then the large green body
Running through the cave.
The night is going to come,
Energy he must save.

Then the swishing tail
Slapping on the wall.
A long, sharp, pointed end
And then he tries to call.

His family now is coming,
Coming to try and help.
They are drawing nearer
As he gives a yelp.

The dragon is now dying,
His food has all run out.
His body is growing weaker,
No longer will he shout.

Rachel Vicars (12)
Daventry William Parker School

CAT

I will start in the dead of night
When the cat is out prowling,
The moon is shining down,
The cat is sitting, scowling.

Then she hears a rustle
In the long, dewy grass,
She aims her small, sleek body
Ready to make a pass.

One more move and she's ready to pounce,
Jumping on the creature
She makes her kill and now she's happy,
That's the cat's main feature.

Daytime dawns, through the small cat flap,
Resting in the cosy house,
Sleeping on the soft armchair
As quiet as a mouse.

Family's down, giving her fuss,
Purring strongly, loudly,
She jumps down to the other cat,
Fighting, rough and rowdy.

Evening comes and the moon,
Waking from her sleep,
Out again, up a tree
Trying to get a peep.

Grace Thorne (12)
Daventry William Parker School

DRAGON

Its bulging eyes big and green,
Always heard but never seen.
It lays in its lair,
Body bold and bare.
Its scaly skin as rough as rocks
As if it's got chickenpox.
It sits and waits within its cave,
Waiting to pounce on its prey.
The beast stirs and once awake
The lives of humans he shall take.
Fiery breath reaches far and wide,
Destroys all it touches and then back
In its cave it hopes to hide.

Laurel Atkinson (12)
Daventry William Parker School

WATER

An outbreak of water from spring to a storm,
The cascades and deepness is about to form
As clear as a crystal beamed in the light.
The upsurge is powerful but still sealed tight,
The rapids rage out like men in a war,
Whirlpools keep spinning more and more.
Hurricanes of water rapidly streak through the air,
The floods and the rapids still don't compare.
The sun has come out and brightly it shone
And there's no more water till the tap's turned on.

Stephen North (14)
Daventry William Parker School

SEASONS

The soft white snow falls gently to the ground
As the trees stand tall and bare.
Snowmen melt in people's gardens
And holly hangs on the doors.

The temperature starts to rise
And the snow begins to melt.
Leaves start growing on the trees
While lambs are being born.

The bright sun shines in the sky,
The heat is rising fast.
All the flowers are in bloom
And the children are out playing.

The leaves start falling off the trees,
The rain begins to fall.
This is the season with lots of colours,
Oranges, yellows, greens and reds.

Siobhan Moll (13)
Daventry William Parker School

THE SEA

Shining blue sea,
Smell of the salty air.
Sea climbs up the golden beach,
Footprints disappear into the golden sand.
Jagged rocks shine like crystals in the bright sun,
Cascading waves sound like a giant thunderstorm,
Sparkling blue sea.

Ashley Davis (13)
Daventry William Parker School

NOT IN OUR HOUSE . . .

Silence falls across the street,
Not in our house.
No one stirs, no one moves,
Not in our house.
The houses are dark, not much is seen,
Not in our house.
We move quickly but also silently,
In our house.
At the midnight hour we flee,
In our house.
We creep in and view our victim,
Not in our house.
We attack their neck, it's strange but true,
Not in our house.
Retreat back in the hour next,
Back to our home.

Katie Moss (12)
Daventry William Parker School

THE LITTLE PET MOUSE

There was an old man who died in a house
But never did die his little pet mouse.
Some say he took it for a walk,
Others say he ate it with a fork.
He had big red eyes shaped like pies,
His big long tail was as cold as hail.
Whatever happened that ghostly night?
The little pet mouse disappeared from sight!

Julie Manning (11)
Daventry William Parker School

NIGHT-TIME

The night is dark,
It is cold,
It's spine-chilling,
My blood's curdling
As I walk down the dark path.

Wired noises,
Terror voices,
Voices mumble
Soft but fast,
My heart is beating faster and faster.

A spooky figure
Moving slowly,
Silhouette making,
Loud howling
All through the night.

Abigail Suthers-Fox (12)
Daventry William Parker School

MONSTERS

The monsters are out in this gloomy night,
They get in a fight
Under the night sky.
They are unbelievably scary,
You are dead.

Liam Hammond (11)
Daventry William Parker School

NIGHT

A gloomy night,
Wind howling,
Trees growling,
Cats miaowing,
Blood trickling while it is snowing,
Dogs barking,
Children running,
Girls screaming,
Babies crying,
Night-time dying.

Mark Thompson (11)
Daventry William Parker School

THE GLOOM

A gloomy night,
A ghostly figure
Silhouetted against the moonlit sky.
I hear strange noises,
Gloomy noises,
Petrified and scared.
I see a shadow behind me,
I look and it has gone,
Then the shadow
Comes back again.

Catherine Hutter (11)
Daventry William Parker School

UNTITLED

Aquatic water crashing,
Torrents whirling around,
Evil water so vicious,
Rapids hurling down,
Water mysteries unsolved.

White horse crashing,
Mist hiding the water,
Cascading water,
Waves crashing down,
Whirlpools hurling water around,
Water mysteries unsolved.

Matthew Payne (13)
Daventry William Parker School

A MISTY NIGHT

A misty night,
Very daunting,
The air is very cold,
My heart starts pounding,
A noise
Louder, louder,
I turn round,
The door opens slowly,
Trapped in one corner,
It is very frightening.

Aimee Roberts (11)
Daventry William Parker School

ORBIT

There was a man
Who was eating an orbit,
He was happy eating in the dark and pouring rain,
But it was a beautiful night,
A quietude night.

The sparkling stars with a sharp curve on the moon,
Which often creeps out after noon,
But the sun came out
And the happiness came out of the man.
The melancholy man twisted
And was never seen again.
But the question is,
Where did he go?

Stella Clarke (12)
Daventry William Parker School

GHOST

The spine-chilling wind blew through my spineless back.
The silhouette trees leant with the wind.
I flew past a forest and the howling of the nightlife
Flowed through my ears.
Terrified screams filled the noise of the cold winds.
When I got back to my shadowy caves
There was nothing apart from a huge hot blaze.
My see-through body started to melt until I was nothing except
A bit of felt.

Adrian Biggins (12)
Daventry William Parker School

MY DREAM ISLAND

My dream island would have a country manor
With 'Welcome' written on one great banner.
I would drive a monster truck
Which would power through all the muck.
I would buy my own football club
And the team would meet in a stinky pub.
In my house I would have a Jacuzzi,
It would make me go all woozy.
I would speed in my speedboat
As long as it would stay afloat.

Tom Lenton (12)
Daventry William Parker School

THE CREATURE

Away up north where the days are short
Lives a helpful creature who wants not to be caught.
Down, down deep in its murky den
It's afraid of the wrath of the cruel, harsh men.
One day it will rise to aid all in need,
Healing, caring and defending if freed
From this treacherous land,
Where the people are damned.
This despairing beast
Will escape far into the east.

Neil Black (12)
Daventry William Parker School

DRAGON

Its big, bold, red eyes stare and stare,
Its body is big as a bear.
It licks its prey until they die,
It then squashes them with all its might.
Its skin is rough and sharp,
It can stab someone in the heart.
Its fiery breath smells so sad,
It makes his prey so bad.
Once he has eaten
He goes back to his cave and hides away.

Lilian Lau (13)
Daventry William Parker School

THE SEA!

Sound of waves against rocks,
Wind rippling the sea's silvery surface.
Sound of cascading water,
Like thunder on a tempestuous night.
Torrential rain hitting the sea,
To make it terrifyingly wild.
The salty rock taste
And white horses galloping along the
Crest of the waves, only to run off,
Then dissipate onto the golden sand.

Carly Brewer (13)
Daventry William Parker School

GHOSTLY NIGHT

It was a spine-chilling night,
A silhouette appeared
And disappeared in a wink of an eye.

The silhouette looked like a phantom,
It was a scary night.
Something touched my back,
I turned around, *aarrgghh!*

Chris Hayward (11)
Daventry William Parker School

AUTUMN

As autumn leaves fall off the trees,
Yellow and orange leaves fall to the ground,
Swirling all around,
They are all around me.

Alex Payne (11)
Daventry William Parker School

GHOSTS

A cold moonless night,
The stars are shining very bright,
In the house of horror
The silent ghosts shine and spread like untidy clutter.

Benjamin Bain (11)
Daventry William Parker School

SKY

The stars are sparkling,
Climbing up into the sky,
Higher than the rain falls,
The moon orbiting the Earth,
The sparkling is fantastical,
The star shape is splendid,
The colours twist in your eyes,
This all happens in the sky.

Hannah Iddon (12)
Daventry William Parker School

SEA (HAIKU)

The vast ocean crashed
And lapped upon the seashore
With seagulls squealing.

Joshua Flynn (11)
Daventry William Parker School

THE SEA

The sea is a dark and eerie place,
It spreads before you deep and blue,
There lives many weird and wonderful creatures.
The waves can change from a ripple into cascading rapids
                                        upon the shore,
With the sun glistening down upon the rocks,
All is calm for another day.

Scott Weaving (13)
Daventry William Parker School

THE SEA

Wind ripples the surface,
Waves come crashing down,
Salty rock taste,
White froth,
Colliding with cliffs,
Ripping up seaweed.

Lewis Hopper (13)
Daventry William Parker School

SPACE

Within the orbit in your eyes you can see
The sparkling stars glistening in the darkness of space,
Stars shaped as the ace of spades,
The moon glowing beautifully and twisting,
Its craters as big as mountains.

Jamie Cleaver (12)
Daventry William Parker School

NIGHT SKY

The sunless sky was sparkling with stars,
Twists and turns of light surrounded the moon,
Curves and lumps on the moon's surface
Makes quietude face of the man on the moon,
His eyes sparkle as he watches over us.

Carlie Morgan (12)
Daventry William Parker School

THE SEA

The sea,
Breaking waves crashing on the golden yellow beach,
Seaweed riding in on the clear surf,
A ship in the burning red sunset,
Flowing on the current,
Two lonely figures sitting watching the mid-summer sun go down,
Spray spitting up cavernous white cliffs,
Sun glistens on the clear water,
The two figures wander through the white surf,
Their footprints are discouraged by the tide.

Thomas Orcherton (13)
Daventry William Parker School

HORIZON

The man walked happily down the road,
The stars were sparkling in the sky,
On the horizon the man was watching the beautiful moon
                                    go up and down.
As he was looking up at the sky he felt the rain climbing down
                                    one by one.
As it got darker and darker the fantastic stars started to disappear
But all he could see was the beautiful moon.
He was saying to himself, I love you.

Victoria Stickings (12)
Daventry William Parker School

WINTER

Winter
White, frosty, cold.
Winter
Sparkles, shimmers, shivers.
Winter
Raindrops frozen on rooftops,
Snow on treetops.
Winter
Ice is slippery.
Winter
Is beautiful.

Louiza White (13)
Daventry William Parker School

IT'S OVER

I've got to say this to you,
I don't know how or why,
Even if you are the star that lights up the night sky.

All the time that we have shared,
The places we went, then compared.
Now all I have to say to you,
I bet you never had a clue
But I've decided to finish with you.

Jamie Smith (14)
Daventry William Parker School

A GHOST

A black murky night,
The moon glitters in the sky,
Cold going through the air,
A noise from my bedroom,
I went in,
Was something in my bed?
Aarrgghh!
It was only my sister.

Clare Gray (12)
Daventry William Parker School

I REMEMBER, I REMEMBER

I remember, I remember,
My 13th birthday,
The cake so big, icing so crisp,
I remember, I remember,
My 13th birthday.

I remember, I remember,
The first day of senior school,
My tie right up, top button done,
I remember, I remember,
My first day of senior school.

I remember, I remember,
The day I was a child,
Those memories so great, so cheerful, so fun.
Those memories all gone.

Shaun Franklin (13)
Lodge Park Technology College

MY MOTHER POEM

M y mother is the greatest
O f all, she is the best.
T he quickest mum in the world.
H er hair is the sun rising.
E veryone likes my mum.
R eady to do the cleaning all around the house.

William Hadden (11)
Lodge Park Technology College

MY MUM

My mum's hair is as smooth as silk
Her eyes are as blue as a clear sky
She is as beautiful as a spring field
Her voice is like a singing robin
Me and her, we do have fun
In the beautiful summer sun.

Jamie Cross (12)
Lodge Park Technology College

MY HOLIDAY

A gain to reunite with
M embers of my large family.
E ating massive cookies
R ound the mall, and then
I   and Milan got lost.
C ousins, brothers and sisters laughing
A t the door of the shop.

Slobodan Manojlovic (13)
Lodge Park Technology College

MYTHS AND LEGENDS

In the days when knights were bold
And dragons lived in caves of gold,
There lived a man called Tom, you see,
He was smiling with a grin of glee.

You see he had just killed a man,
He stole his money, then he ran.
He must be punished, someone thought,
He found a man of the magic sort.

The wizard delved into his purse,
He waved his wand and said a curse.
Tom, his legs were stuck like glue,
He swore and cursed without a clue.

He shouted loud, 'I hate this day,
I do not want this curse to stay.'
He wriggled around like he was having a fit,
But it didn't work, not even a bit.

'Okay, okay, I'll do what I can,
I confess, I killed this man.
Just take this curse away from me,
Just help me please, I beg, I plea!'

The wizard picked up his wand again
And led Tom to his secret den.
He locked him in a dragon's lair
And gave young Tom a mighty scare.

So Tom had made a sacrifice
Instead of his legs being in a vice,
He decided to spend the rest of his years
Confronted with his greatest fears.

Joshua Weston (12)
Lodge Park Technology College

MY LIFE

Here I sit alone in my bed,
My life is speeding past,
Visions of my youth pass through my head,
As I sit here alone in my bed.

My younger years,
Playing at home,
Before growing up and going to school,
The large building is one huge rectangular dome.

My teenage years,
Growing older and taller,
Getting extra homework from school,
My friends suddenly look smaller.

My adulthood,
Spending years at college,
Trying to get a good job,
Using all of my knowledge.

My middle years,
Now I have children,
To cherish and love,
But they soon will also have children.

My old age,
I have many grandchildren to play at my feet,
Now that my wife has gone they brighten me up,
Whenever I see them across the street.

Now I am alone,
My children are older and have moved away
And I will be lonely,
Until my dying day.

Graham Abraham (13)
Lodge Park Technology College

WAR ON TOKYO

On the shore killing some more,
Bullets are flying, people are dying,
Shooting my gun, having some fun,
Shooting Japan, lost a man.
Shooting a plane, starting to rain,
There blows a pillbox from my friend fox,
We feel like a yo-yo, Alpha go go,
Tanks go up the beach killing Japan like a leech,
Firing good, not too bad, come on you can make it lad.
We're on the warpath, pillbox in sight,
Island of fear is here tonight,
Blood everywhere, it's giving me a scare,
Climbing to the top, better not stop,
Shot a sniper, want his gun so I can shoot Japan just for fun,
We've won the war with dead people on the floor,
There's our flag, with a big cheer, I could do with a cold beer.

Aarron Young (13)
Lodge Park Technology College

THE GIRL OF MY DREAMS

Tonight as I go to bed, I dream of a girl.
A girl with long, silky blonde hair and skin as fresh as the sea.
Her face is as beautiful as a flower.
I hope sometime we meet, along an exquisite beach
As the sun sets and birds are flying over our heads.

I wake up and the girl of my dreams is gone.

Luke Robinson (11)
Lodge Park Technology College

MY GARDEN!

I'm five, sitting on the grass in the garden,
The ground starts to shake
And suddenly I'm not in my garden, but in the jungle.
The trees and plants have grown hundreds of feet
And the tip of space they meet.
The ground is warm and damp,
The trees whisper, 'Explore, explore,'
I look around with such intensity, that I don't see where I am going.
I step on the cat, she growls like a tiger, then runs off to where water
is flowing.
The moon starts rising,
I start realising,
That the jungle is a bad place to be,
When it's only me.
There's a rustling in the bushes
And the moon throws the clouds away with its pushes.
I look around, nothing in sight,
Only the moonlight.
Suddenly, a tiger leaps from the bush,
I get pushed against a tree,
Knowing there is only me,
The tiger leaps towards me.
'Emilly,' my mother calls,
Now I'm back, sitting on the grass in the garden,
I run up to bed fast, to finish the dream
And although it may seem,
Only a dream,
In my heart it will always be a jungle.

Emilly Savage (14)
Lodge Park Technology College

DESKS

Desks,
So much history,
I woz ere and ere woz me,
Jamie loves Laura,
Wait and we'll see,
Cute little stickmen
As funny as can be.
And under the desk
A rainbow of gum,
Not soft and squidgy,
But hard and numb.
This desk shows some history.
I woz ere and ere woz me.

Michelle Kingsnorth (12)
Lodge Park Technology College

TOWN'S GLORY

Ipswich Town are my fave team,
They're not as bad as they seem.
Sometimes they draw and lose a lot
And they don't score with every shot,
But when they win that crucial game,
It makes me lose all my shame.
They're not doing well in division one,
But I think they need to start having fun,
Then they might win some games
And all the fans will light their premiership flames.

Jamie Haynes (13)
Lodge Park Technology College

THE WORM

There's a worm in the bottom of the garden,
I tried to throw it in the bin.
It's all wiggly
And jiggly
And sits there on its own.
It's always all alone,
Listening to the boring drone
Of the mower moving to and fro.
It never moves, it's round and long,
Always singing the same song,
'Flubber, lubber, flubber flu.'
I want to throw it down the loo.
It escapes me every time,
But oh no, not this time.
One sunny afternoon
I brought it to its doom.
I was gardening one day
And it decided to play.
It wriggled in the soil
As I started to boil,
'Oh no, look out!' I cried,
But it was too late.
My turning fork moved right
And gave the worm a fright
As I cut it in *two!*

Danielle Macleod (12)
Lodge Park Technology College

NO WORD OF A LIE

I have been to Mars and that's no word of a lie.
I am 104 on Saturday and that's no word of a lie.
My mum is the Queen and that's no word of a lie.
I can count to 2 million in 0.3 seconds and that's no word of a lie.

I have 125 trophies and that's no word of a lie.
You don't believe me, do you?
All right, all right, all right.
I'm the biggest liar in the school and that's no word of a lie.

Sam McKinnon (11)
Lodge Park Technology College

BREAD

I make bread in the morning,
I make it every night.
Whenever I look at bread,
It's love at first sight.

In sandwiches I love it best,
I've got jams of all sorts.
Chocolate, honey, plain old butter,
Best served with knives and forks.

I bake it, make it, eat it,
I love it through and through.
Eggy bread I love the best,
It looks like loads of goo.

With fry-ups I have fried bread,
I sometimes have soggy toast.
I have bread with everything,
Even with Sunday roast.

I love it, I love it,
Oh yes, I love bread.
And yes I always eat it,
I don't care what everyone said.

Kieren Burt (12)
Lodge Park Technology College

CHRISTMAS TREE

I'm
a little
Christmas tree,
tall and proud, I have
lots
of shiny
tinsel, but I'm not
very loud, sometimes I get sad
when
I'm locked
away, but when I pop
my head out, kids have a lot to
say.
Underneath
me are the presents
all sizes big and small, I see
people
wrapping
and I
quite
like
them
all.

Zoe Wood (11)
Lodge Park Technology College

RAIN

Rain is so high
In the sky.
It's never dry,
I don't know why.

When rain hits the ground
It makes a splashy sound.
Splish-splash all around,
Rain splishes and splashes then rebounds.

Remi McNeill (12)
Lodge Park Technology College

SPRING!

Spring
is a time
when
flowers grow.
Instead of freezing,
the wind will just blow. Butter-
flies flutter in the
blue skies. In
a field a
little lamb lies. At
night I like
to look
at
the moon
but don't
for-
get
it's
sum-
mer
so-
on.

Samantha Fulton (11)
Lodge Park Technology College

AGE

What do you see children?
What do you see?
Are you thinking
When you're looking at me?
A crabbit old man
Just simply dumb
Oh! Look at me
I've hurt my thumb,
I didn't used to be old
I used to be young
Young oh! Young!
That's when I had fun
Now you see, children
Now you see
I am not
I cannot be me,
I was free and fearless
Nothing to do
Now look at me
Surrounded by you.

Peter Stewart (13)
Lodge Park Technology College

MY MUM

My mum is the best, she's great,
My mum is my best mate.
She looks like a princess and is one too,
There's not much my mum can't do.

Her eyes are blue, her hair is brown,
She cheers me up whenever I'm down.
I'm just glad I got the best
And I wouldn't change her for any of the rest.

My mum is great in every way,
That's why I tell her I love her every day.
My mum is the greatest ever,
Hopefully she knows I will love her forever.

Fiona Campbell (12)
Lodge Park Technology College

GRANNY

What do you see?
What do you see?
Are you thinking
When you look at me?
A wrinkly old woman
With grey frizzy hair
Always nagging
'What you doing over there?'
Telling old stories
About many years ago
Never knowing what to do,
Always going to and fro
Who never remembers
Like a silly old fool.
Who am I kidding?
I'm not cool.
Always stopping for a rest
My bones are creaking.
Everyone is saying,
'That Granny is reeking.'
Is that what you see?
Is that what you think?
Then open your eyes
And try not to blink.

Stacey McFarlane (13)
Lodge Park Technology College

WHEN I WENT TO WEMBLEY

The day had come it was time to go
I put my clothes on I was ready to go
I ran out the door as fast as lightning
So sat I in the car waiting, then my dad
Started the car and off we went.

We finally reached Kettering, I got
Out the car and crossed the road
Went in a pub and bought a coke
Sat down and read an article on Homer
Then the bus came, it was time to go.

I jumped out my seat and ran out the door
Got on the bus and picked a seat, the
Bus started and everyone started to
Cheer. Two hours later we were in London.

The bus parked up, I ran in the stadium
I ran down some steps, got our seats
Sat down, I started to eat, the game
Got started, then *goal* the other team
Scored.

Twenty minutes later *goal*, we scored
Everyone went crazy, then *goal*, we
Had scored again. We were finally winning
Then the ref blew his whistle, it was half-time.

The second half got started after 15 minutes
Goal the other team had scored, it was 2-2
The game was nearly ending, then *goal* the other
Team had scored again. That was the end

The ref blew the final whistle. The other
Team won the cup. I walked out the stadium
We got on the bus, then the long journey
Started, to get home.

Lewis Lang (12)
Lodge Park Technology College

GRANDPARENTS

(In loving memory of Kaye Laws, April 1945 - February 2003)

G reat friends
R eally caring
A lways there when you need them
N ever unhappy, always smiling
D on't ever give up
P repare fun and games
A lways fun
R eally hip and cool
E ventually they will go
N ever to return
T hen you'll regret unspent time
S omeone really important

Are your grandparents.
Always spend time with them,
and you will never regret loving them
like they love you.

Sierra Wilson (12)
Lodge Park Technology College

POEM

I split my head open and it was very sore,
They stitched it up, and I couldn't ask for any more.
My first game of footie, it was really cool,
I played my first match, at Studfall Junior School.

My first day at Lodge Park, it was so bad,
I'd rather have had a day off, 'cause it was driving me mad!
My worst lesson, was definitely French, it was really boring.
First of all I fell asleep, then I started snoring!

Everytime I play for the school,
We always win, I'm never a fool.
The team at Lodge Park, they are good,
They play the game like they should.

My first holiday was in Paris,
I went to see the team Clarisse.
I have also been to Portugal,
All the people there are really small!

This is my poem,
This is the end.
This is great,
I win again!

Jordan Middleton (12)
Lodge Park Technology College

MY BEST FRIEND

My best friend is Jemma Neal,
She sleeps on a banana peel.
She doesn't realise when she does,
She's as crazy as a rabbit going buzz.
She does not go to Lodge Park, but the CTC.

I like her and she likes me.
Her pet is one rabbit called Jet, she even wants a dog.
She likes the names Rosie and Mog.
She's my best friend in the whole wide world,
Her hair is short and straight, not long and curled.

Heather Currie (12)
Lodge Park Technology College

ROBOT

Flashing lights
On   the   cold
Metal   machine
The enormous
Bicentennial thing
Lurches
Towards
Me
As the strong monster tries
To battle the ugly creature
He twists and turns and then
He strikes the creature down
It curls up in a pool of slime
The robot slides away into the

d	t
a	h
r	e
k	n
n	i
e	g
s	h

of   s   t sky

Lewis Mathew (11)
Lodge Park Technology College

MY LIFE

M y birthday had come
     and I was one,
     I was so full of joy and fun.
Y ears later, I was five.
     I started the infants' school,
     I thought it was very cool.

L ater on in life,
     I started at the junior school.
     They read me books on ghosts and ghouls.
I whizzed through the junior school
     And got through to
     Lodge park school.
F ive bits of homework a night,
     I've experienced my first flight,
     To Gran Canaria.
E nd of my school life
     is on its way,
     I can't wait to sing and shout *hooray!*

Hayley Elliott (13)
Lodge Park Technology College

ABOUT ME

I'm small and delicate like a china doll,
Six months old and growing fast.
I've got a soft rabbit that I love to hold,
My mum wants this moment to last.

My first day at school was extremely daunting,
Miss Clark helped me learn and grow.
My time at school was speeding by,
Now I have to wear a tie.

I'm a teenager at last,
In the senior school,
The years have soon passed
And I think that's cool.

Alison McAuley (13)
Lodge Park Technology College

WHAT DO YOU SEE?

What do you see, Paul,
What do you see?
What are you thinking
When you're looking at me?
An old fragile wife
Or the person inside me?
The young girl you married?
Tell me what you see.
I once was a young girl of ten,
Carefree with two older sisters,
Nothing could stop me then,
Nothing, I say nothing.
I'm now 16
And still young at heart,
I'm still in my teens
So please don't call me old.
I now am married at 20
To a handsome young man,
I hope I stay with him until the end of the century.
His name is Paul and he's a thoughtful young man.
Now at 25 I have young of my own.
Two of them just like their dad.
They're lucky to have a loving home,
With a loving dad and a loving mum.

Sarah Millar (13)
Lodge Park Technology College

A BORN HERO

Britain's idol, he's a hero,
He means so much to us.
He's such a fashion statement,
He always makes a fuss.
Front pages of the papers
Are where he's always seen,
For a new haircut, or his family.
Then it comes to Saturday
Where he is the star,
It's his favourite day,
He is the best by far.
A family to be proud of,
A loving wife and kids,
They're always there when needed,
He's always in the mix.
He is a born hero, such a raw talent,
He is our very own, David Beckham!

Jordan Gourlay (13)
Lodge Park Technology College

MEMORIES

I remember, I remember,
When I was younger,
We were moving into our new house,
Our whole family were very excited.

I remember, I remember,
Stepping into my new room,
The sun shining through the windows,
Thinking how brilliant it will look.

I remember, I remember,
My mum and dad decorating my new room,
I remember looking at it,
It was fantastic.

Kerry Green (12)
Lodge Park Technology College

MY BOX
(Based on 'The Magic Box' by Kit Wright)

In my box . . .

Is the famous gold jewellery of Egyptian kings.
In my box is the great Rosetta Stone.

In my box . . .

I have control of immortality.
In my box I can fly up to space
because I won't need a spaceship.

In my box . . .

I have the Stone of Destiny.
In my box I can turn into a water creature
when I go into water.

In my box . . .

I have control of memories from the past, present and even the future.
In my box I can climb the highest mountains.

In my box . . .

I can jump up to space and touch the stars.
My box is encrusted with gold all the way round
And has the richest coloured velvet.

Alastair Graham (11)
Lodge Park Technology College

MEMORIES

I remember, I remember,
Standing in the wind,
Seagulls quarrelling loudly
and the sea roaring in the wind.

I remember, I remember,
toppling overhead,
I landed on my side,
I thought I was dead.

I remember, I remember,
lying on the sand,
blood on my leg
and on my hand.

I remember, I remember,
later in the day,
my body covered in plasters,
as I sat in the bay.

Simon Sherwood (12)
Lodge Park Technology College

MY MUM

Her hair is dark as the night,
Her eyes are brown and bright,
She is the one that is always there,
With lots of loving care.

So beautiful and sincere,
She is always near,
She makes me laugh
Because she has a funny-looking scarf.

She takes me out,
All about,
She is the one that always helps me,
That's because she loves me.

Gemma Hemmings (12)
Lodge Park Technology College

THE MAGIC WORLD OF MY DREAMS!
(Based on the poem 'TheMagic Box' by Kit Wright)

In my box . . .

I wish I could swim with dolphins,
across the cool, deep blue sea
and surf the underwater nation,
as they join up together joyfully.

In my box . . .

I wish that I could become famous
and make new songs each day,
with all my friends and family cheering me,
as they watch me play.

In my box . . .

I wish that I could go to school more
and learn each day a new thing,
to become more educated
and to know about each living thing.

In my box . . .

My dream is to live in the sea
and to look after all the creatures
and to make their life worth living for,
so they can see different natures.

Symone Rust (11)
Lodge Park Technology College

THAT GLORIOUS VENTURE

It is of that glorious venture of war that I write.
That venture that destroys innocence, virtue and humility.
That venture that inspires men to greatness in the most evilest of ways.
That venture that sees young men crawl, stagger and suffer in forgotten fields in distant lands.
That venture that sees men run into the abyss of death, where bleak darkness reigns yet it is said the most honour found.
War, that venture that is said to build nations and sustain freedoms yet destroys the values they seek to behold,
These countries who may regain after arms are laid to rest but whose values are forever corrupted.
War fought in the preservation of civilisations where our souls are sold unto the Devil, and so no man shall ever win a war, rather lose it to forever remain embittered upon its struggle.
Be it soldier, general or citizen, that glorious venture shall forever corrupt.
War, that glorious venture.

Lee Butcher (15)
Lodge Park Technology College

COLOURS

Colours can be dark,
Colours can be bright,
They can be glow in the dark,
So they show at night.

Various shades of blue,
They're not all the same,
They can all be blue,
But they have a different name.

Colours can be light or dark,
There are all different kinds,
Colours sometimes have a mark,
They're all easy to find.

Colours can be cold,
Colours can be hot,
Colours can be bold,
Colours, there are lots.

Lucy Wilkinson (13)
Lodge Park Technology College

THE OCEAN

Not on the land but in the sea,
There is a city no human eyes have seen.
It's more glorious than we can imagine,
Beneath the sea where it all began.
First the corals of great magnitude and power,
Their colours so bright shine through the sea.
The great shoals of fish in a radiant shower
Make the silent water ripple with their rainbow scales.
Next come the people who live a the heart of the ocean
And care for all around them, they are the merpeople.
The most beautiful of all the merpeople is their queen,
With hair as red as fire, eyes as pure as the deepest ocean
And her heart of solid gold.
Like the ocean from where we all come,
She sits there with her underwater kingdom of beauty,
The ocean!

Roxanne Heath (12)
Lodge Park Technology College

YEAR TO YEAR

When I was one, I could sit and crawl,
When I was two I was still very small,
When I was three I had my first pram
And my dolly's name was Sam.

Now at four I have started school,
Learning to read and write.
I have made lots of friends
And we like playing in my den.

Now at ten, my last day of juniors',
Teachers and pupils all say goodbye.
Life goes so quick,
I stand and sigh.

Off to America with my family,
Mickey Mouse, Donald Duck and all.
At the age of eleven this was a dream,
Although I was very small.

I'm a teenager now, thirteen years old,
There are some things I cannot be told.
My aim is to do well, I think I will do well,
But only time will tell!

Jodie Douglas (13)
Lodge Park Technology College

MY MUM

My mum's lips are as red as a rose,
Her hair is as soft as silk.
Her eyes are bright like the moon,
Her teeth are whiter than snow.
Her smile is priceless to me.

When my mum's sad, I feel sad.
When my mum's happy, I feel happy.
I feel her heart reach out to me.
That's what my mum means to me.

Janine Johnston (12)
Lodge Park Technology College

GREY WOMAN

What do you see nurses,
what do you see?
What are you thinking
when you're looking at me?

An old grey woman with
a wrinkly face who cares
what you think, you
think I'm a disgrace.
I'm puny and small
you don't care at all.
You look in my eyes,
you bring me mince pies.

Why do you hate me . . .
Hate me so much?
My mum has died
I can feel her touch.

I was 16 and very keen
I didn't like teachers they were mean
I was a child once
with a mum and dad
a mum and dad I could have had.

Laura Hunstone (13)
Lodge Park Technology College

In My Box

(Based on 'The Magic Box' by Kit Wright)

In my box . . .
I shall swim with dolphins and
incredible fish in the bright blue sea.
Be the queen and rule the country
and live in the palace, in London.

In my box . . .
I will catch a star and
cherish it forever.
See my family that have
passed away.

In my box . . .
The birds will join me
and help me fly in the sky.

In my box . . .
I shall surf the oceans,
live underwater and
look after the creatures.

Nikolina Manojlovic (11)
Lodge Park Technology College

My Best Friend

My best friend's really funny,
He likes to get straight in,
He doesn't think about things much
And has a sparkling grin.

I've known him since we both were kids,
We've fallen out sometimes.
We always end up making up,
It's getting hard to make this rhyme.

Sometimes when I'm all alone
And no one's coming out,
I wish that we were brothers
So we could play and shout.

And so this poem has to end,
To keep it short and sweet.
My best friend's called Liam
And I think he's really neat.

Alexander Thomson (13)
Lodge Park Technology College

FEELINGS ABOUT MOVING SCHOOL

When I got up this morning,
I was nervous, scared and sad.
When I went downstairs this morning,
Everyone drove me mad.

When I arrived a the school gates this morning,
Everyone stood and stared.
When I walked through the yard this morning,
No one looked like they cared.

When I got to the form room this morning,
One girl looked at me.
When I sat down in my chair this morning,
She looked like she was my enemy.

When I went home this afternoon,
I was nervous, scared and sad.
When I stormed upstairs this afternoon,
Everyone drove me mad.

Nicolina Bosnic (12)
Lodge Park Technology College

THE GRAFFITI DESK

The desk used to be smooth, square and straight,
But now the corners are rounded and drawn on with hate.
Malicious, cruel minds drawn on with words,
But others are soft, not rounded, but squared.
Look, here's one now, a graffitied word, 'Jay 4 Haz',
I wonder who they were?
Moving my eyes across the worn desk,
More and more names like 'Randell 4 Tex.'
Looking across, there's 'Jab 00' and
'Nics 98' and 'Caz 4 Joe',
'Hayley 4 Burton', 'Mark 52',
Andrew and Moe were other names too.
I scanned the desk looking at names,
Like 'Debs 92', 'Aaron' and 'Holmes'.
I looked and looked at all the words,
Some were rude and squiggled with hurt.
Others were soft, kind, round things,
But some have a weird kind of tinge.
The names all around started to blur,
But something stood out, some softened words.
I looked down at the test I was about to write,
Then thought of the words, the words that said,
'Take flight.'

Rebecca DeRosa (12)
Lodge Park Technology College

REAL LIFE

I remember, I remember
My mum's first wedding.
They made me wear a suit that I was dreading.
Then at the party they made me sing and dance.
Then my dad sang loads of old pants.

Two years later at the christening, the water on my head was glistening.
Then my brother started to cry.
Then he became really shy.
Now he is 8 and I am 13 and we live in a nice little house.

Mark McGoldrick (12)
Lodge Park Technology College

IN MY LONELY OLD AGE

There are lots of memories
That race through my mind,
Like where did all the time go?
And why can't I find
Somebody who can see me as what I am
Behind this wrinkled old face?
Why do I have to remind
Them that once I was young?
No one ever lied
They told me I could do anything -
I really could, now it is a lie
I cannot do things anymore
Even if I tried!

When I was a woman of 30
If I strained my mind,
I remember my two children
My husband by my side.
But at an older age of 73
There's no one left to comfort me,
So can't you see?
That I need
You love, your help, your company.

Heather Millar (13)
Lodge Park Technology College

MY MAGIC BOX
(Based on 'The Magic Box' by Kit Wright)

In my box I will have . . .

A ghost as white as a sheet.
A boy flying around the world.
Three silver sparks from a lightning bolt.

I will have in my box . . .

A gust of wind from a lightning bolt.
A shower of cats and dogs falling from the sky.
A molten rock from an active volcano.

I will have in my box . . .

A sip of the bluest water in the world.
Four silver wishes hidden in the corners.
A dinosaur from the Stone Age.

My box . . .

Sides will be made of gold.
The lock and hinges are made of fire.

Shaun Wilson (11)
Lodge Park Technology College

HIPPIES

H ippies are everywhere
I   n my life.
P op over here and a
P op over there,
I   t all becomes one, but
E nds with a flare,
S o hippies vanish with a pop into thin air.

David Skewis (11)
Lodge Park Technology College

WHAT DO YOU SEE?

What do you see, nurses
What do you see?
Are you thinking
When you're looking at me.
A lonely old lady
Sipping her tea?
What do you see, nurses?
Tell me, what do you see?
One day
I was young.
One day
I had fun.
I'd play with my brother
And sit in the sun.
I used to be able to swim a mile
Nowadays I get cramp if I walk to the shop.
I could bend over backwards,
Now I can't even hop.
I'm all alone
My husband is dead
And I lie here
Lonely in bed.

Hannah Clelland (13)
Lodge Park Technology College

THE SNAKE

It slides and slithers then swims in rivers.
It slithers and slides gives you a fright then runs and hides.
It slides and slithers and gives you the shivers.

Jamie Catalano (11)
Lodge Park Technology College

MY DAD

Dark brown hair and big brown eyes
loving cuddle with a lovely smile
floats about without a care,
sometimes here, sometimes there,
always busy but has a flair,
that's my dad and I won't share.
He's the best, he's number one,
me and him have loads of fun.
He makes me laugh and
he makes me smile,
we can only be apart for a while.
Yes, he is my dad, he's number one,
I would never trade him for anyone.

Kristina Stoner (12)
Lodge Park Technology College

IF I HAD A . . .

If I had a pet dolphin
I would treat it with love and care.

But if I could fly I would
fly over the world.

And if I had a waterfall
I would love to feel the water
dripping down my neck.

But if I had a rocket
I would fly into space
blasting off in my rocket.

Gemma Till (11)
Lodge Park Technology College

ANGEL

At the bottom of the garden, what can you see?
An amazing bright light behind the tree.
A radiant beauty came into view,
The first thing I thought of was, *who are you?*
The creature came forward and whispered in my ear,
'Listen deeply and what can you hear?'
I listened and listened and still heard nothing,
But then I listened harder and heard a harp playing.
Beautiful music flew through the sky,
I stared at the creature and asked her, 'Why?'
I looked at her and she was so small,
She listened and stared but said nothing at all.
Then she rose up very slowly and said,
'I'm an angel and that's not a lie.'

Emerald Nightingale (12)
Lodge Park Technology College

MY WONDERFUL WORLD

My wonderful world would be a treasure trove
of weird and wacky ideas of only my inner imagination.

I would create a waterfall of fire and a blaze of water.

An ever-growing oak tree and a golden eagle to guide me.

I would create a mountain of gold and a fountain of land.

I would create an identical world in an identical universe,
with identical stars and moon.
So that not only I could gaze at its glory.

Christopher Marshall (12)
Lodge Park Technology College

LIGHT-SPEED DUCK

When there were heroes good and bold,
There was a great one, I've been told,
I saw him in my dream last night,
Battling in a fantastic fight.

There always is a villain though,
This one is extremely slow.
His partner is completely white,
He was joining in this fight.

The slow one though you must see,
His name was Slo-mo-bee.
His partner would give you a fright,
You know, the one who was completely white.

Moon Man was this one's name,
He was searching for a path to fame.
He wanted to kill the hero, you know,
Light-Speed Duck, he's not slow.

Joe Doherty (12)
Lodge Park Technology College

MY MUM

M y mum is the best,
O f them all,
T he greatest mum in the world,
H er hair is like fire,
E veryone loves her,
R apidly she does the housework around the house.

Sarah King (11)
Lodge Park Technology College

FRIENDS!

Everyone needs a friend,
To be there for them until the end.
To make them smile when they feel down,
To feel for you when you're around.
To help you with your troubles,
Joined at the hip, they are your double,
Friends are cool, friends are smart,
They are your life,
They're in your heart.
When you're lonely, feeling blue,
Friends are there to comfort you.
Your friends leave memories in your mind,
Keep them with you, don't leave them behind.

Keri Bethel (13)
Lodge Park Technology College

DOLPHINS

D   olphins are lively and fun.
O   ther people think differently about dolphins.
L   iving creatures are cool.
P   erhaps dolphins are like us because we swim.
H   er fin is thin.
I   love dolphins.
N   ormal dolphins are fun and kind.
S   pecial dolphins are cute.

Ashleigh Burrows (11)
Lodge Park Technology College

COLOURS

Colours are dark,
Colours are bright,
Colours shine all day and night.

What's your worst?
What's your favourite?
Nobody knows but you.

They can be different sizes
And different shapes.
They can glow in the dark
Or shine in the light.

There are hundreds in the world,
There are millions in the universe.
What's the one that will suit you?

Katie Dickson (12)
Lodge Park Technology College

HIDDEN POEM

H   is for hidden, hidden you can't see.
I   n the deep, dark, damp earth, damp as can be.
D   ents and dips in the Earth.
D   ark and damp as we all can see.
E   mpty and hollow as you can see.
N   aughty people hurting other people.

Colin McGreevy (11)
Lodge Park Technology College

EARTH BOUND

E arth's dug up from a ditch of the dead,
A body pushes it way out and reattaches his head.
R ivers of tears trickle down his beloved farm as he approaches
  his loudly crying mum.
T ired and weak he steadily walks and suddenly hears a hum,
H ears the humming of the cornfield, it sounds like the corn fairies.

B ooks his mum read made him happy, but thinking about it made
  him sad. Oh he loved his mum, dear Mary.
O wls hoot in the dark and the damp.
U nder the trees and on the porch, he slips and grabs on the lamp.
N ervously, his mum opens the door and sees what the loud noise is,
D eadness appears in front of her and she falls into the arms of his.

Daryl Veal (13)
Lodge Park Technology College

MY MUM!

M y mum smells like fresh flowers picked from a peaceful garden.
Y ou know when she is around because she makes you feel very
                                                welcome.

M y mum is like a big, soft, cuddly bear.
O f all the mums, she is number one.
T he whole world knows my mum.
H er voice is like an angel singing.
E verybody loves her.
R emember her because she is a special star.

Lucy Mackenzie (12)
Lodge Park Technology College

ANIMALS

Dogs can be big or small,
they like playing with a ball.

Cats have short hair or long
and sometimes they can really pong.

Snakes are long and look very slimy,
some you see you think, cor blimey!

Pigs are fat and mostly pink
and most of the time they really stink.

Bulls can be very grand and large,
when they see something red they like to charge.

Elephants are big and strong
and their trunks are very, very long.

Animals on the whole are different creatures,
all shapes and sizes and different features.

Paul Britton (12)
Lodge Park Technology College

MY MUM

M   y mum is very kind.
O   f the people in the world, my mum is the best.
T   he skin of my mum is so soft.
H   er hair feels like silk.
E   veryone in my house admires my mum.
R   elying always on my mum, because she is trustworthy.

April Jackson (11)
Lodge Park Technology College

PEANUT BUTTER

There are hundreds of ways of getting peanut butter
Off the top of your mouth.
You can scrape it off with your fork,
Or maybe scrape it off with your spoon,
Or even scrape it off with your finger.
There are hundreds of ways of getting peanut butter
Off the tip of your finger.
You can scrape it off with your knife
Or wipe it on your plate,
Or even scrape it on the top of your teeth.
There are hundreds of ways of getting peanut butter
Off the top of your mouth!

Mark Burton (13)
Lodge Park Technology College

RAINBOW

Blue is the sky that gives us light,
Yellow is the sun, shining bright.
Green is the grass beneath my feet,
Red is the flame, burning in the heat.
Brown is the tree, standing tall,
Violet is the bird flying over all.
Orange is the sunset laying in the sky,
Indigo is the petal, growing as the day goes by.
All these are colours of the rainbow.

Ryan Stewart (12)
Lodge Park Technology College

THE CLASSROOM DESK

I open my eyes and see large, bold words
Carved in the desk with hate and hurt.
I move my eyes left and right,
The words are small beyond my sight,
But here are two in the left hand corner,
They say, 'Caz is great' and 'I love Lorna.'
Here's one now, it's messy and scribbled,
It's been written in Tipp-ex, white and dribbled.
Why do these people indent their words
And make their comments so absurd?
Is it boredom? Is it spite?
Defacing property, they have no right.

Nicola Howden (13)
Lodge Park Technology College

FOOTBALL

Football is a sport usually played by men,
The number of players is one more than ten.
They run round a pitch, poor old souls,
But it's worth it when you score a goal.

Two popular players are Beckham and Owen,
This is when it comes to showing
Their skills against another team,
But sometimes it can end up mean.
Man U are the best by far,
I have to say all eleven are stars.

Joanne Beaton (12)
Lodge Park Technology College

SPAGHETTI

Spaghetti, twisting and turning on a plate,
It spins in and out of your fork,
It hangs off a cliff, longer than a rope,
Gliding in the wind.
It's like a snake twisting in and out,
It's like blood on a vampire's mouth, dripping
Down his lips all through the night.
It twists through your fork like
A headphone wire spinning in your fingers.
It looks like hair, rough and tight.
Spaghetti, mmmmm . . .

Alexander Lyon (12)
Lodge Park Technology College

EYES

Eyes are brown, eyes are green
Some are soft and some are mean.
You can tell by their eyes if they're going to lie,
Some are crystal-blue, like the sky.
Some are false, some are fake
Like the colours pink and opaque.
When you think your eyes might blink,
If we didn't have eyes, what would we do?
You wouldn't see me and I wouldn't see you.

Hayley Muir (12)
Lodge Park Technology College

EYES

Eyes, eyes everywhere,
All they do is stare, stare, stare.
They stare at you in the night
And when it's dark they give you a fright.
Hazel, blue, brown or green,
Wherever you are you're gonna be seen.
From up above or down below,
Eyes can see you wherever you go,
So don't try to hide because you'll always be seen,
Wherever you go, they'll know you've been.
If we didn't have eyes, what would we do?
So beware, because they're watching you.

Gail Sheridan (12)
Lodge Park Technology College

MY MUM

My mum, she is caring
She likes sharing.
My mum is the best,
Better than the rest.
When I'm bad,
It makes her sad.
When I'm sad,
She makes me feel happy
Because she's my mum.

Dusan Knezevic (12)
Lodge Park Technology College

My Mum, My Mum

Her eyes as blue as the shiny sea.
Her teeth as white as the winter snow.
Her skin is as smooth as a freshly polished table.
Her hair is like the waves of the sea.
Her smile is worth a million pounds.
Her shout can erupt a volcano.

Katie Jones (12)
Lodge Park Technology College

Mum

Her face is as bright as flowers,
Her eyes are as blue as the ocean,
Her hair is as yellow as sunflowers,
Her hug is as warm as the sun.
That's my mum, I love her!

Carly Black (13)
Lodge Park Technology College

The Hospital

Patients panting in pain,
The aged, dark hospital again -
A musty smell upon the air,
More people start to arrive.
Rude people push to the front,
Polite people sit there with bloody limbs.
Millions of doors in the building
But not as many doors as floors.

Leanne Booth (13)
Manor School

BEHIND THE LENS

Scenes of devastation were nothing new to him -
He thought himself professional and detached.
To keep his camera steady
He had learned long ago to overcome
Fear and compassion while working.
Again and again his lens was faced with death.

But this was different, very different.
Not since his first assignment
Had he felt such shock and helplessness.
As what seemed, at first, to be a tragic accident
Turned out to be a sinister, cold-blooded massacre
On a scale he had never witnessed before.

A year on and he was back.
He paid his respects at Ground Zero like everyone else
To prove to himself and others that he cared.
This time his shots were more sedate
In a calm, peaceful atmosphere;
Though his hands shook more than they ever had before.

Ian Flanagan (16)
Manor School

LOVE'S DAMNATION

With crimson wings bestowed by Love upon life
Would I fly, were it not for legs of lead.
Oh but how the cold rapier of my strife
Doth reap the chasm whence I may not tread.
But should I stand on yonder bridge of gold,
Would burning hells of my heart consume me
And cast me down into bitterness untold,

Binding me with thorns for eternity.
The pain and anguish shall I lock away
In the sanctity of my soul's darkness,
Where then my heartstrings shall forever fray
By the daggers slicing from cold harshness.
Yet with such words on my tongue can I finally see,
That the binding chains are born within me.

Chris Ovenden (15)
Manor School

THE GRAVEYARD

The wind scraped past gravestones blowing flowers,
Shooting them up to the musty sky.
Its dreariness hit me cold,
No colours, grey and drab.
A cloud hovered like a helicopter over this shadowy place,
Sun in the surrounding area enclosing the space.
My eyes wandering from stone to stone,
Glimpsing till locking onto familiar names and imagining their faces.
My emotions took hold, thinking happy thoughts to block out the
                                                   harrowing ones.
I walked on.
My knees trembled as I stepped, jumping over lumps of earth,
Forced up from the bodies that took its place.
Stopped, stared, grey marble lay dull when it once shined,
Gold lettering glistened despite no light.
It was a familiar grave,
As I read it, cold shivers ran up my spine.
I darted out towards the exit.
I jumped out,
In the split-second I felt the sun,
A glow of ecstasy came over me.

Karen Britchford (13)
Manor School

FRIENDS AND FAMILY

Friends and family
Are all I need,
They make me laugh,
They make me cry,
They make me eat things I don't like,
Like meat and vegetables, yuk!
But sometimes they let me eat
The things I like,
Like pizza, chips, yum!
Chocolate, cakes, yum!
Christmases and birthdays
Are really cool,
Presents and gifts galore.
I don't know what I'd do
Without my friends and family,
So let's make the most of it,
While I've still got so many.

Charlotte Johnson (13)
Manor School

MY OLD STREET

My old street;
No one nice to meet,
Street light has broken,
Quiet, no one has spoken.

I wonder why and why again
At weekends it had to rain.
Why did I feel so glum?
I wondered when I'd see the sun.

Streets are filled with drunken kids;
Streets with rubbish, bottle lids,
People coming from the pubs,
Streets with cans and Pringles lids.

I ask myself, did I live here?
A neighbourhood, this neighbourhood.

Kathryn Wieczorek (13)
Manor School

GUILT!

I'm sitting in my room,
Tears dripping from my eyes,
Thinking long and hard
About my hatred and despise.
She's silent in her room,
But I can hear her pain and sorrow,
Maybe if I leave her there
She'll have forgotten by tomorrow.
You should have seen her eyes,
They said, 'What kind of mum are you?'
For those were the words
I'd once said to my mum too.
And what about the scar?
That will take some time to heal,
No, not the visual scars,
But the one that she can feel.
I'm sitting in my room,
Tears dripping from my eyes,
Thinking long and hard
About my hatred and despise,
Not for her . . . but for myself.

Charlotte Bramble (13)
Manor School

DOWN AT THE PUB

Down at the pub are two men drunk;
Singing and dancing with no soul or funk.
A pint of Fosters and a Smirnoff Ice,
The barmaid drinks vodka with a lemon slice.
A nice hot curry and another pint or two,
All night long they'll need the loo!
Up on karaoke 'Star Trekking' they sing,
Looking for a bird to have a little fling.
A game of pool to win a bet,
Another beer they will get!
As the cash runs out, they start a tab,
It's closing time, so they call for a cab.
But oh no, they're out of money,
They stagger home, laughing as if something's funny.
In the morning headaches arise,
No crimes committed, or is that all lies?

Jemmer Parnell (13)
Manor School

THE SHED

Rusty nails lay in a pile
Like orange leaves on an autumn day.
The tools on the shelf looming in the dark
And the tins of paint piled in a corner.

The dark gloom of the roof,
The slow rumble of tools,
The creaking of old planks
And the thud of a hammer hitting metal.

The old shed I like it so much,
It creaks and squeaks,
Soon it must be knocked down,
It will be a shame to see it go.

Oliver Tatum (13)
Manor School

TREE

Tree,
Helpless tree,
Standing innocently,
Standing in the park.
Watch,
Watch the people,
Watch them mess it up.
The branches,
broken.
The trunk,
Unattractive.
The graffiti,
Some 'work of art'.
The squirrels, birds,
Scared.
The children,
Playing, climbing, swinging.
The next day,
Same again.
Just leave it be.
The poor,
Helpless,
Innocent
Tree.

Jack Maddix (12)
Manor School

ALTON TOWERS

Lots of loop-the-loops,
Shakes you side to side,
Some smooth, some bumpy,
Some in dark of night.

The illusion of Hex,
Fastness of Black Hole,
Wetness of the log flume,
Shock of the haunted house.

Some are slow,
Some are fast,
Some make your bones shake
And some make you sick.

In the dark,
In the light,
All you can hear
Is childrens' fear.

Natalie Medforth (13)
Manor School

YOUR VASE

I am sorry that your vase is broken,
I just knocked it and it smashed on the floor;
I got you a drink, just as a token,
You yelled at me and threw my drink at the door.

I wanted for us to be friends again,
You told me to get out of your sight;
You threw me out into the pouring rain,
I ran off into a cold winter's night.

I came round to your house the next morning,
I offered you your favourite flowers;
You sent me packing, with a very stern warning,
You didn't smile, you only glowered.

You sent me a very lovely letter,
Hoping this would make it a bit better.

David Smith (14)
Manor School

THE DAEDALUS AND ICARUS POEM

Feeling like a prisoner in the land called Crete
Was the man called Daedalus we're about to meet.
His story is sad, but very true,
Hating his life and not knowing what to do.

One fine day while looking up in the sky,
He had the idea, I'll make myself fly.
He gathered feathers, pipes, reeds and other things
And in no time he had made perfect birds' wings.

His young son Icarus was standing by,
Watching his father, not understanding why.
He couldn't go and leave his son there,
So he made some wings as perfect as the other pair.

The day had come, they were ready to fly,
Daedalus told Icarus, 'Don't fly too high.'
Not knowing their fate, they flew through the air,
Icarus flying as high as he dare.

Tragedy strikes. Icarus flies too near the sun,
His father gasps, 'What have you done?'
Icarus has drowned, never to be seen again,
Daedalus looks on, his heart full of pain.

Kayley Dickens (12)
Manor School

LOVE IS, LOVE CAN

Love is a budding flower, reluctant
to prove itself. A suffering: intense
as the moonlit midnight sky. An ocean
so deep and infinite, it covers the
entire universe and moves only
with its loved one. Love is the light at the
end of the tunnel. It protects you from
evil and brings you through the darkest days.
Love cannot be stopped by any living
organism, its strength overpowers
all life on Earth. Love can move anything
that stands in its way, it can overcome
the highest mountains, climb the highest walls
and swim the deepest, darkest oceans.

Emma Dixon (15)
Manor School

ME

I want to be,
I want to see,
I want to know how to be me!

I want to be,
I want to see,
I want to find out what it is like to be she.

I am she,
I am me,
I am happy to be just me!

Emma Yates (12)
Manor School

Love Is . . .

Love is a meaningless walk through the dark
that lets you in without even warning,
but won't let you go, it plays with your heart,
makes prey of you, to catch when hunting.
Love is a strong wind that takes hold of you,
early it lasts, but not returned dies down.
If who shows it has their passion's love true,
the love twists them and of them makes a clown.
So let's say our love, it's dealt by Cupid;
a blind little nude man with wings, bad aim,
a small stumbling man with arrows. Stupid.
Love should be handled properly. A game?
Why should love be a curse? A bad treatment?
Love is fine for two, for one: punishment.

Luke Beardmore (15)
Manor School

Christmas

December the 25th, the best day of the year,
The hint of happiness in the atmosphere.
Snow on the ground, turkey cooking,
Look at Santa he's really good-looking.
I wake up early and see presents under the tree,
If only some other people are as lucky as me.
The world is a mess, full of greed,
Why do people want things they don't need?
The smell of Christmas dinner, mmmm smells good,
After we've eaten it, it's time for Christmas pud.

Carina Henderson (13)
Manor School

LOVE SONNET

Love is something no one can touch or see,
The feeling of being great and small in one,
The flower that draws in the misguided bee,
A power as needed and wanted as the sun.
No contract binds two people as love does,
Nothing can prepare for what love makes us feel.
When it is gone, you can't define what it was,
But love can be broken as can a deal.
Love can be given up, or worse still, lost
And there is nothing that love cannot do.
To give up your heart is the only cost,
You may end up giving your life though, too.
Love can bring happiness, love can bring joy,
But don't treat love as if it is a toy.

Jade Simms (15)
Manor School

MY DEAR COMET

Oh comet of the starry and open sky,
I ask you why people must die.
I'll tell you one I have kept in my head,
That is that they fear you, they fear they are going to end up dead.
I hear you laugh aloud and say,
'I am going to hit the ground today
And they will be dead. They will be dead! They will be dead!'
But, my dear comet, will you ever learn to apologise?
I don't know, but that's for you to fear.

Katherine Lewis (12)
Manor School

The Basement

The faded light shining through the barred windows,
Barred as if to keep something in.
Slowly walking down old steps,
Every other one broken,
Putting your hand out
For the handrail,
Only to get that dreaded splinter.

Looking around at your surroundings,
Not quite sure if you saw something move,
Then the only light source,
The door creaks,
Then encores with a loud slam.

Reaching out in the dark,
Feeling for the light,
Click, there it's on,
Flickering, but on.

Seeing what it is you wanted,
Slowly moving along
The slightly slippery,
Hard, harsh floor.

The light's gone out,
You can see nothing,
Smell nothing,
Hear nothing, apart from
Your pounding heart and panting breath.

Then you realise,
You're in the basement
On your own in the dark.

Jasmine Jamieson (13)
Manor School

THIS IS A DREAMWORLD . . .

The world is a place of peace,
Serenity and happiness.
No one argues or shouts,
Wars do not exist at all,
Now they are just vague,
Distant memories.

No longer shall we struggle
Through poverty and disease.
Never shall we pollute
And destroy our planet again.
No more wasted time in traffic jams
With fumes reaching out to destroy.

This is a dreamworld,
Can this ever exist?

Everything is recycled,
Helping the world
That is what we do.

No more travelling and polluting,
We do it all friendly
And clean and not
Hurting anything.

This is a dreamworld,
Can this ever exist?

Katie Harrison (13)
Manor School

YOU ARE MY FEAR...

I'm normal really, honest I am,
I look like all of you,
Two eyes, two ears and a nose,
I am just like you,
Why am I different?
Why do I have to hide?
I dread leaving my home,
Somewhere I hardly ever have to hide,
I try and stay in the light,
You only get me in the dark,
You only scare me on my own.
Two eyes, two ears and a nose,
That's you, that's me,
I close my bedroom door, switch the light off,
That's when you come, you scare me.
'Stop!' You don't listen,
I switch the light on and you've gone, why is it me you choose?
You make me afraid of the space around me,
Why is it I can't live without you being there?
I am just like you,
Two eyes, two ears and a nose,
I am just like you,
Yet I'm scared, *you are my fear.*
I am just like you,
Except, I can see right through you,
I guess I can say, you're a ghost,
I cannot hide forever,
I am just like you,
I'm - just - like - you!

Krystina Freeman (14)
Mereway Upper School

WHAT IS LOVE?

Love bring happiness, tears, confusion,
Blissfulness, heartbreak, mystery,
Secrets,
Lies,
Kisses.

The sea-salty tears that are dried
By the gentle, soft touch of a lover's smooth kiss,
The great happy smile that is fed
By the return of a loved one,
The mystery that is solved
By the easing words of someone close.

Love is strong, love is powerful,
Love is almighty, can tear you down,
Can lift you up.

Love is open
To anyone who needs it,
To those who want it,
Yearn for it,
Desire it.

Love is for all, but not all can have it.
Love can be dangerous,
Exciting.

Take it,
Have my love,
Fulfil my dreams,
My deepest desires.

Hold me, kiss me,
Don't ever make me sad,
Love can turn.

It can hurt as much as it can relieve.

What is love?

Hannah Steele (15)
Roade Comprehensive School

My Body

It's my soul carrier,
My shell,
My frame,
It makes me, me.

It carries my organs,
It's slim and slender,
It carries me around.

It has a variety of poses,
It's as short as an alarm clock
And as smooth as a scaly snake.

It's flexible and bendy
And fit enough to ride.
Its heart's like gold,
It's my friend.

My body and I.

Connie Carver (13)
Roade Comprehensive School

CALABODE

Hidden in the forest, a mother spins a tale,
The stories never told but once and never growing stale.
The mother tells of Calabode, her red hair flowing softly,
A river flows, but silently, its willows old and lofty.

Beneath the twinkling star-spread night,
Beside a fire glowing,
A younger girl, she lies awake,
The warm west wind is blowing.

And as the years go by with time,
The stories seeming smart,
The mother still as young as night,
The wild mushroom tart,

But through the moonlight in the glen
Yet moonbeams bright as any day,
The mother starts up yet again,
With stories that will never stray.

The mystical Knight of Calabode
Upon his pony Eire,
Has married Princess Amarode,
A maiden, sweetly fair.

But when the fires' embers fade,
The younger is asleep,
The mother with her story made
Too closes her eyes for sleep.

And with another tale ended,
Another chapter closed,
Another hole which has been mended
In this story with no woes.

There will always be a Calabode . . .

Katie Coyle (16)
Roade Comprehensive School

I THINK MY SISTER'S AN ANIMAL

She has a hyena laugh when I make a mistake,
I feel like screaming, 'For goodness sake!
Soph, you annoy me again,
Crikey girl, you're such a pain!'
Her magpie tendencies are simply absurd,
My sister has the brain of a bird,
She is always stealing my stuff
And if I complain, she just says 'Tough!'

Like a cockerel she's up at the crack of dawn,
Not a moan, a grumble, or even a yawn.
When I'm still asleep, it's time for lunch,
How she gets up, I don't have a hunch!
Like a snake she slithers to my room unseen,
Knocking my computer and smudging the screen,
Slowly, silently, secretly sneaking,
Doing so much without even speaking.

Raiding the fridge for a midnight feast,
Is she a person, a bird or a beast?
As sly as a fox she can make up a reason,
Whatever the time, the day or the season.
If you walk past my house you may simply ignore,
A squeak, a hiss or maybe a roar,
But keep to the path, whatever you do,
It may look like a home but it's really a zoo!

Emma Fry (12)
Roade Comprehensive School

HORSES

Jodphurs, hat and gloves to take,
Straw and muck I've yet to rake.

I like horses and they like me,
They often seem like family.

Soulful eyes and soft hair,
A spirited nature beyond compare.

They have style and they have grace,
More than our human race.

Today it's Humphrey that I've got,
A rolling gait and sedate trot.

Cantering is such fun,
Though galloping is number one.

Feel the wind rush past your ear,
Smooth and fast, without the fear . . .

That you'll end up rolling in the mud
When you fall and land with a thud.

A cousin of the horse could easily throw you,
Stopping sharply, just 'cause he wanted to.

Horses are sweet and gentle as a rule,
Though watch out for that trace of mule!

Cheryl Spick (14)
Roade Comprehensive School

THE DIFFERENCE

You don't need a shoulder to cry on,
I do.
You don't feel ashamed of yourself,
Do you?
You don't get laughed at by the kids at school,
You're not clumsy, or a fool.
You don't sit at home trying to find
The reason why your mum and dad left you behind.
You don't keep asking yourself if they're going to come back.
I know deep down they won't.
I keep telling myself they will,
But they won't.
That's the difference between you and I.
You're perfect.
Someone who's perfect is hard to find.
I'll never be perfect,
I just can't accept it.

Gemma Roberts (12)
Roade Comprehensive School

THE BRIDGE

For centuries the bridge be safe,
but aaaaallll of a sudden it ain't.
Folks be agasp to see the signs in paint,
but lying there beneath the bridge
be the most hhhhhorrible sight
it be the dreaded *Trollive!*
That gives these folks a fright.

Tom Falkner (12)
Roade Comprehensive School

TRAVELLING THROUGH SPACE

Space is so lonely
And not a sound of a word,
Only an explosion
As a comet hits planet Earth.

The unknown passes by me
And pretends I'm not there,
So I carry on travelling
Through the darkness of space.

As I pass the stars and the planets,
A beautiful sight in the distance
As a supernova occurs.

The fear, the horror,
As death draws near.
The explosion expands
And draws near.

Kerryn Stoppel (13)
Roade Comprehensive School

DARKNESS

Children of the beast embrace
To scorn and hate the human race.
Consume the light that hugs the Earth
And aid the wounded in giving birth,
A group that will appear
And guide you through this final year.
The dark armies then will come,
When the darkness is for one!

Jamie Craigie (12)
Roade Comprehensive School

LOST IN SPACE

Suspended in space
Floating freely,
Missing my mum,
Dad and dog,
Will we win?
Lost, lonely, loathing life,
Angry aliens all around.
Sadness and silence surrounds, suffocates,
Sad stories about silence in space,
Shooting stars, sun, sky,
Unhappy, unending, unearthly,
Detesting dreadful darkness,
Loving luminous light,
Cannot cope,
Bitterness badly breaking me,
Deprived, distressed - will death come?
Everlasting evil, eternally never-ending,
Terrifying, troublesome, tiring,
Ghastly, ghostly, gloomy shadows,
Horrifying, hateful, horrendous habitat,
Hope is held; Hell must end,
Food will fill me finally,
Water will wake me wondrously.

Rhian Owen (13)
Roade Comprehensive School

A SPECIAL FRIEND

There are funny feelings spinning around in my head.
Something I haven't told you,
Something I haven't said.
You are there, you are the one who made me see love.
You are my special friend sent from above.
You are my love, my little treasure,
You are my best friend, I will love you forever.

Jessica Cowley (12)
Roade Comprehensive School

FRIENDS

Friends, friends, what can you say
When they're down your house, you want them to stay.
When I'm sad they cheer me up,
By saying 'Ramsgate' or 'Whasssssup?'
They come to me about their problems
And of course they help me with my sums.
I trust them with anything; we all have a laugh,
I love them 100% plus a half.
We all love parties, especially discos,
We all love singing, especially Clo Bo,
Supporting each other is important to me,
It's important to someone else, that's Mitzy.
Shaz, Hannah, Jess, Clo Bo, Kim and Sam,
There's even more, do you think I can?
Well, there's nothing like your friends,
It's a thing that never ends.

Bhavika Nayee (12)
Sir Christopher Hatton School

HALLOWE'EN

Children doing trick and treat,
Long nose witches, smelly feet,
Wriggly snakes and gooey eyes,
Broomsticks flying in the skies.

Hallowe'en is here,
You're in for a scare,
Hallowe'en is here,
I bet you wouldn't dare.

Pumpkins staring at you all night,
If you dare you're in for a fright,
Getting bags full of sweets,
Yummy, yummy snakes to eat.

Hallowe'en is here,
You're in for a scare,
Hallowe'en is here,
I bet you wouldn't care.

Scary and creepy facial masks,
Eyeballs floating in a flask,
Children sick before they go to bed,
Time to rest our pumpkin heads.

Claire Stancliffe, Laura Waples & Matthew Marks (13)
Sir Christopher Hatton School

BLACK LOVE

Our love was fun when we first met
The best love that anyone could get

Our happiness lasted for days and days
Your lovely smile and your cute little ways

I thought that for once my joy would last
And not end up like things in the past

My friends were all jealous of what we had
To them getting a girl was only a fad

Soon after that things took a turn
Unfortunately a lesson I had to learn

I waved goodbye with a tear and a kiss
Your gentle nature was something I'd miss

This is the meaning of the words 'black love'
Letting go of my angel sent from above

How am I supposed to survive and live on
When all that I've been living for, is gone?

Since then in my heart I've cried and cried
It wasn't our love, but you that died.

Kirsty Wilkins & Chloe Hamilton (13)
Sir Christopher Hatton School

September 11th

Country against country
Guns and the talk of war,
People plotting sinister plans,
The issuing of threats,
The evil is rising.

Fire, fire, dust and debris,
People stand horrified,
Screaming their last before death,
Their last wishes unfulfilled.

People jump for their lives,
Flying like angels through the air,
Firefighters down on the ground,
Praying for survivors.

Families grieve over the losses,
Memories are all they have,
The looks on their faces,
How happy they once were.

One year on,
The heartache still continues,
Their lives have been destroyed,
And as the way is cleared
The last tear falls on Ground Zero.

Jodie Clark & Kelly Smith (13)
Sir Christopher Hatton School

MY FAMILY

Talitha, my sister, is small.
When she is fun it is cool.

Joshua, my brother, is too rough,
He is big, strong and very tough.

Ben, my brother, is only 10,
But he can drive me round the bend.

Lee, my brother, is irritating,
Always me he is imitating.

Bobby, my brother, is very stressy,
Especially when his hair gets messy.

Jacqui, my mum, is tall and blonde,
Of all of us she's very fond.

Gary, my dad, is big and bald
And by all of us cannot be fooled.

Charlotte Lawrence (12)
Sir Christopher Hatton School

THE SEA

The sea with wild blue colours
Clashes against the rocks,
As people bring in their boats
And stand upon the docks.

The sea creatures flowing in the water,
Swimming to and fro,
No doubts or worries, just swimming
Around and so . . .

There is something about the sea, you know
And you can be there for evermore,
It doesn't matter where you are,
Along the coast or along the shore.

Lucy George & Hannah Reed (12)
Sir Christopher Hatton School

SCHOOL-CHILDREN HATE THAT!

Peanuts and stressy teachers
Teachers say you lovely creature
School-children hate that

Teachers nag, shout and bore
And when you're naughty you go out the door
School-children hate that

Homework's hard, boring and bleak
Homework's only fun for a geek
School-children hate that

But every child's worst lesson is history - boring
Especially first thing in the morning
School-children hate that

You're best friend's gone on holiday
Lazing round the pool
While every single schoolchild
Is stuck at boring old school
Everybody hates school!

Lee Wager (12)
Sir Christopher Hatton School

HAPPINESS

Happiness is love
Though the grass isn't always green,
It can't be dependent
On a life that has been.
It could be a time
Where your heart is full of content
Or a life through which
You carry no regrets.

Brightened by the weather
When it's a cloudless, sunny day
But your mood can soon drop
When the sky is dull and grey.

To me a simple comfort
From a person close and dear
Can lift my spirits highly
Things are then a bit more clear.

So happiness is hard to define
It could be many things
Although affected by the world
It's yours to choose in the end.

Tanya Mercieri (13)
Sir Christopher Hatton School

LOVE

Love is the thing a little bit more than friendship,
Love is the thing most people know.
The only problem I can think of is everybody wants it.
The only problem is that there is no love left for me.
Love must be clear as far as the eye can see,
But love is not always clear.

It has its ups and downs.
Love has its smiles,
Love has its frowns,
But now all I can do is wait for she
And wait for love to find me.

Christopher Cox (13)
Sir Christopher Hatton School

A SIMPLE LIFE

Day is when the sun shines bright,
Beaming down a wondrous light.
Lying as the clouds go by,
Gazing dreamily into the sky.

Evening comes and night draws near,
The world of darkness is now here.
The night is lit up with the moon and stars,
In the black outer space near Neptune and Mars.

Clouds are swirling round and round,
Looking for shapes we haven't found.
The burning heat of the sun comes down,
Reflecting across from town to town.

Wandering through a lonely street,
There is no one for us to meet.
As night comes we go to bed,
Taking the thoughts right out of our head.

Whatever happens during the night,
Or even during the day,
Don't let it hang on your mind,
As tomorrow is on its way.

Andrew Marsh (14)
Sir Christopher Hatton School

HATRED!

Hatred is something we could all do without,
Hatred makes us scream, *hatred* makes us shout.

Envy takes over, we don't know what to do,
Envy makes us wannabe like you.

Love tries to build a perfect Earth,
Love like a baby from a new birth.

Anger is *hatred* when it is expressed,
All those around soon become depressed.

Evil we find is the root of us all,
It does not help us when we want to stand tall.

Friends should help us through our bad times,
They're there for our wins and for our crimes.

Hatred is something we could all do without,
Hatred makes us scream, *hatred* makes us shout.

Jake Hill (13)
Sir Christopher Hatton School

DEATH

Death
It's something that we all fear
Especially when it comes so near
Feeling scared, frightened too
Wondering when it will encounter you

Death draws near when you grow old
The last bit of life is what you hold
Lying there, full of sorrow
Thinking of what soon will follow

After death where will you go?
The answer to that no one does know
Some believe that you'll live on
Others think that you'll be gone.

Keith Tate (13)
Sir Christopher Hatton School

A KID'S LIFE

I can hardly believe the last day of term is finally here,
Tests, exams, all that stress, oh it's been such a long year.
I'm fed up of writing, of reading too,
Especially the books I feel have no relevance,
Although the teachers insist they eventually will.

The children are happy, the teachers as well,
It's the beginning of summer and I know it's gonna be swell.
Late nights and lie-ins are both to come,
So are holidays abroad, and relaxing in the sun.

You can see your friends whenever you like,
Go with them to exciting places, or just to the park on your bike.
There's shopping, the cinema, swimming in the open air,
When the summer soon ends, it won't be fair.

September arrives far too quick,
Back to reality, it's enough to make you sick.
Roll on Christmas, the season of good cheer,
It will soon be the end of another good year.

Shelley King (12)
Sir Christopher Hatton School

BEST BUDDIES

Best buddies always best,
Playing football and the rest.
Hamsters - Sammy and Nigel,
Making a big poo pile.
Listening to music at school,
Which we think sounds really cool.
We like getting our dosh,
And eating our nosh.
We like riding our bikes,
And going on long hikes.
Science is easy,
Whereas maths is easy peasy.
Always there for each other,
Getting each other out of bother.
Joining up as a double,
Getting us into trouble.
Best buddies always best.

James Carswell & Andrew Grimmitt (12)
Sir Christopher Hatton School

DREAMS

I always wished to be a star,
Shining bright without a care,
Looking down on everyday life,
Up there where the air is fair.

I always wanted to be an actor,
With the high life in my palms,
All the money I could want,
Girls swooning in my arms.

If I could be a doctor,
Helping people would be my dream,
Help those that are ill or sick
To fulfil their own dreams.

James Nightingale (12)
Sir Christopher Hatton School

SHOPPING

I like lots of shops
And I like lollipops,
I like Northampton,
Shopping there is cool.

Now I go there,
I have funky hair,
Make-up too
And underwear.

Mk One is the best,
It's better than all the rest.
T-shirts here and trousers there,
I never have enough to wear.

Miss Selfridge shop is neat,
Shopping there is a treat,
The clothes are cool, the gifts are fab,
But I won't be seen there with my dad.

New Look is great
When shopping with a mate.
With Mum it's a chore
And always a bore.

Kimberley McGee (12)
Sir Christopher Hatton School

BETRAYAL

I hate the way you broke my heart,
You took my soul and tore it apart,
You stood there right in front of me,
You didn't care that I could see.

You hurt me and you made me cry,
I walked away and wanted to die,
I needed my friend, she wasn't there,
She was running her fingers through your hair.

There was one person - a true friend,
My broken heart she tried to mend,
But through all this I still couldn't see,
You were the fool it wasn't me.

Now I know it was your loss,
And you will have to pay the cost,
I've moved on and left you behind,
Now my heart I have to find . . .

Abbey Wiggett (13)
Sir Christopher Hatton School

I SAID . . .

I said we could
He simply said we couldn't
I said we must
He straightforwardly said we mustn't
I said it wasn't fair
He sternly said it wasn't
I said I loved him
He sadly said nothing
I said I hated him
He slowly walked away.

He said he was sorry
I said I understood
He said he didn't mean it
I said I too, felt that way
He said he really loved me
I said that I did too
He said let's be together
I said me and you.

Katie Adams (13)
Sir Christopher Hatton School

FUNKY FRIENDS

True friends are always about,
They will always be there to help you out.

When you're sad,
They will never be mad.

They won't mind,
They will always be kind.

We will always be together,
Best friends forever and ever!

You are a friend that is true,
I will always be there for you.

I've known you since you were one-year-old
And will definitely know you when you are going bald!

This is a friendship so pure,
It will last forever, I'm sure.

Bethany Lawrence & Shannon Chivers (12)
Sir Christopher Hatton School

NIGHTMARE

Nightmares,
My greatest enemy,
They have no weakness,
Have no flaw,
It sees my weak spot
And rips it raw.
Has no fear,
Sheds no tear,
Has sharp eyes,
Of massive size.
It has rancid breath,
Scares me to death,
My every heartbeat it hears,
But best of all,
It disappears!

Simon Lymn (13)
Sir Christopher Hatton School

DREAMY NIGHT

D   o you know what you dreamt last night?
R   eality or not?
E   lapse the time away
A   s weird as they are,
M   aybe they are connected with
Y   our conscience!

N   ight life passing by
I   rregular they are
G   oing to places you never thought possible
H   aving no control
T   he meaning will soon come.

Amy Fothergill, Megan Hayes (14) & Lydia Ashley-Clarke (13)
Sir Christopher Hatton School

GIRLS AND BOYS

G irls are lush, girls are muck, some smell nice, some smell yuck
I like blondes, I like browns, I like smiles, I like frowns!
R ed bra, black bra, no bra, ohh ahh!
L oving boys all day long, wearing their bright blue thong!
S ad and happy, dumped and single, but when she comes back
she makes me tingle!

B oys are cute, boys are fine, young like orange, old like wine!
O h so silly, aftershave, nasty deodorant, so last week's rave.
Y ellow, pink, purple 'n' lime and this poem doesn't rhyme
S ad and happy, dumped and single, but when he comes back
he makes me tingle!

Alex Waller & Jack Chopping (12)
Sir Christopher Hatton School

RE-ENACTMENT

R e-enactment battles
E ngaging the enemy
-
E ntering the arena
N ever give up until you get shot
A cting out the past
C oming down the hill
T anks rolling in
M en running everywhere
E nemy firing from their positions
N ow being shot at
T ime for the battle to come to an end.

Bradley Hartshorn (12)
Sir Christopher Hatton School

SEPTEMBER 11TH 2001

Never again shall we forget,
The thousands lost that day.

Never again shall we forget,
The panic caused that day.

Never again shall we forget,
The tears that flowed that day.

Never again shall we forget,
The mayhem caused that day.

Never again shall we forget,
Falling paper,
Ferocious fires,
Hijacked planes.

Never again shall we forget,
Pictures of two planes,
Crashing into the side of the
World Trade Centre.

Never again shall we forget,
The heroic firefighters who gave their lives,
To let others survive,
'Because of your daddy,' mothers will say,
'Other daddies came home that day.'

Never again shall we forget,
September 11th 2001.

Simon Mayes (13)
Sir Christopher Hatton School

LOVE IS TRUE

How romantic
Is love?
Let me tell you:
A feeling
Held dear,
The light
At the end of the dark tunnel,
A thing only you can see
Apart from the one
Who loves you back,
The memories
You treasure and keep,
Love is your all
Your everything,
The time the clock
Stops working.

It can turn
Out badly,
It can cause
Grief
Anger,
Leaves you
Hanging on . . . and on . . . and on,
The key to all
Emotions
Opening your heart
To those who know you.

Ceri Lewison (13)
Sir Christopher Hatton School

IS IT ALL A DREAM?

Sun smiling down on Earth,
Gives heat and light,
Warm, comforting smile,
Hearts are lifted.

Birds tweeting,
Beautiful voices laugh,
World bright and joyful,
Holidays in the sun.

Dead, cold, stone moon,
Dim silvery light covers the land,
Spooky shadows creeping around,
Mysterious voices whispering.

Twinkling stars of mystery,
Waterfalls of afar,
African rainforests of beauty,
Galaxy, a space of dream!

What are dreams?
Mind games or wishes?
Memories, or thoughts?
Or . . . what's meant to be?

Sun smiling down on Earth,
Gives heat and light,
Warm, comforting smile,
Hearts are lifted,
    Is it all a dream?

Adam Dale (13)
Sir Christopher Hatton School

CRUEL LOVE

Dig the knife a little harder,
You back-stabbing jerk.
This love isn't blossoming flowers,
But dagger-edged stems of the rose,
Slashing blindly at our hopes of happiness.

Hold me a little tighter,
My cuddly teddy bear,
Our love is like a gift,
A burning desire, a deep passion igniting
In the warm, breezeless nights.

Dig the knife a little harder,
You self-absorbed loser,
This love is made of false hopes
And the beginning of a road to endless
Tears, fights and the persistent pain.

Hold me a little tighter,
My warm, kind-hearted love.
Our love is like the distant humming bird
On a morning of glorious light,
As the forever golden sun rises over our lives.

Dig the knife a little harder,
You cold and heartless liar.
This love you don't deserve
For I am tired, like the petals of a weeping rose
And as it dies, so too does my love for you.

I love you more than words can express,
Yet despise you, for this empty void you have left!
My heart has cried endlessly, for you and only you!
So now I must say,
Goodbye, you self-absorbed loser: my cuddly teddy bear.

Fiona Veal (13)
Sir Christopher Hatton School